# Celebration of Life

Pregnancy Organizer and Journal

Presented To

___

Given by

___

Date

___

Occasion

___

Freeman-Smith, a division of Worthy Media, Inc.
134 Franklin Road, Suite 200, Brentwood, Tennessee 37027

*The quoted ideas expressed in this book (but not Scripture verses) are not, in all cases, exact quotations, as some have been edited for clarity and brevity. In all cases, the author has attempted to maintain the speaker's original intent. In some cases, quoted material for this book was obtained from secondary sources, primarily print media. While every effort was made to ensure the accuracy of these sources, the accuracy cannot be guaranteed. For additions, deletions, corrections, or clarifications in future editions of this text, please write Freeman-Smith.*



Cover Design and Page Layout by Richmond & Williams, Brentwood, TN

ISBN 978-1-60587-374-9

Printed in the United States of America
1 2 3 4 5—SBI—16 15 14 13 12

*A perfect take-along companion to help you record all the necessities of your pregnancy.*

A DIVISION OF WORTHY Publishing WWW.WORTHYPUBLISHING.COM

# Introduction

*As a mother comforts her child,*
*so will I comfort you . . .*

—ISAIAH 66:13 NIV

Because you've picked up this book, it's safe to assume that congratulations are in order: you're expecting a baby. This organizer and journal is intended to not only help you record all the special moments of your pregnancy, but also to remind you that God will accompany you and your baby throughout your pregnancy, during the birth, and throughout eternity.

Each section has a quote, inspirational thought or verse that will help bring you closer to the One who has blessed you with this baby. There are sections to record appointments, how you feel physically and emotionally, special prayers for your little one, and eventually all the details of your special day when you meet your child!

Hannah Whitall Smith observed, "How changed our lives would be if we could only fly through the days on wings of surrender and trust!" During the exciting days ahead, remember to trust God each day. Allow Him to guide you, to protect you, and to lead you through, and then beyond your pregnancy. The days will fly by and before you know it, your precious little one will be here!

Take comfort in the fact that the Creator of the universe stands ready to protect you and your baby today, tomorrow, and forever.

# Contents

# Journey Expectations

What I hope to experience during my pregnancy and first moments with my baby...

# Journey Expectations

What I hope to experience during my pregnancy and first moments with my baby...

Week One Date: ____________________

## Daily Encouragement

*This is the day the Lord has made; let us rejoice and be glad in it.*

PSALM 118:24 HCSB

Appointments today: *Doctors/Dentist/Hair/Nails/etc.*

What I'm feeling in my heart and spirit:

What I'm feeling physically:

What I ate today:

What I weighed today: ____________________

Daily "to-do's": *shopping/errands/home tasks/etc*

Memorable Headlines or Event of the Day: *(current event from the news or in my own life)*

**Baby Countdown: 39 weeks to go**

Due Date: ____________________

Week One Date: ____________________

## Daily Encouragement

*The Lord God of heaven and earth, the Almighty Creator of all things, He who holds the universe in His hand as though it were a very little thing, He is your Shepherd, and He has charged Himself with the care and keeping of you, as a shepherd is charged with the care and keeping of his sheep.*

HANNAH WHITALL SMITH

Appointments today: *Doctors/Dentist/Hair/Nails/etc.*

What I'm feeling in my heart and spirit:

What I'm feeling physically:

What I ate today:

What I weighed today: ____________________

Daily "to-do's": *shopping/errands/home tasks/etc*

Memorable Headlines or Event of the Day: *(current event from the news or in my own life)*

**Baby Countdown: 39 weeks to go**

Due Date: ____________________

WEEK ONE Date: ______________________

## DAILY ENCOURAGEMENT

*Be anxious for nothing, but in everything by prayer and supplication, with thanksgiving, let your requests be made known to God.*

PHILIPPIANS 4:6 NKJV

Appointments today: *Doctors/Dentist/Hair/Nails/etc.*

______________________

______________________

What I'm feeling in my heart and spirit:

______________________

______________________

What I'm feeling physically:

______________________

______________________

What I ate today:

______________________

______________________

What I weighed today: ______________________

Daily "to-do's": *shopping/errands/home tasks/etc*

______________________

______________________

Memorable Headlines or Event of the Day: *(current event from the news or in my own life)*

______________________

______________________

**Baby Countdown: 39 weeks to go**

Due Date: ______________________

WEEK ONE    *Date:* ____________

## DAILY ENCOURAGEMENT

*May your day be fashioned with joy, sprinkled with dreams, and touched by the miracle of love.*

BARBARA JOHNSON

Appointments today: *Doctors/Dentist/Hair/Nails/etc.*

______________________________

______________________________

What I'm feeling in my heart and spirit:

______________________________

______________________________

What I'm feeling physically:

______________________________

______________________________

What I ate today:

______________________________

______________________________

What I weighed today: ____________

Daily "to-do's": *shopping/errands/home tasks/etc*

______________________________

______________________________

Memorable Headlines or Event of the Day: *(current event from the news or in my own life)*

______________________________

______________________________

**Baby Countdown: 39 weeks to go**

Due Date: ____________

WEEK ONE Date: ____________________

## DAILY ENCOURAGEMENT

*As a mother comforts her child, so will I comfort you . . . .*

ISAIAH 66:13 NIV

Appointments today: *Doctors/Dentist/Hair/Nails/etc.*

What I'm feeling in my heart and spirit:

What I'm feeling physically:

What I ate today:

What I weighed today: ____________________

Daily "to-do's": *shopping/errands/home tasks/etc*

Memorable Headlines or Event of the Day: *(current event from the news or in my own life)*

**Baby Countdown: 39 weeks to go**

Due Date: ____________________

## Personal Journal

You know my heart Lord...

## A Mother's Prayer:

Precious baby, I pray for you, I care for you, I love you...

Week Two Date: ____________________

## Daily Encouragement

*We must lay our questions, frustrations, anxieties, and impotence at the feet of God and wait for His answer. And then receiving it, we must live by faith.*

KAY ARTHUR

Appointments today: *Doctors/Dentist/Hair/Nails/etc.*

What I'm feeling in my heart and spirit:

What I'm feeling physically:

What I ate today:

What I weighed today: ____________________

Daily "to-do's": *shopping/errands/home tasks/etc*

Memorable Headlines or Event of the Day: *(current event from the news or in my own life)*

**Baby Countdown: 38 weeks to go**

Due Date: ____________________

Date: ____________________

## Daily Encouragement

*Every morning he wakes me. He teaches me to listen like a student. The Lord God helps me learn…*

ISAIAH 50:4-5 NCV

Appointments today: *Doctors/Dentist/Hair/Nails/etc.*

____________________

____________________

What I'm feeling in my heart and spirit:

____________________

____________________

What I'm feeling physically:

____________________

____________________

What I ate today:

____________________

____________________

What I weighed today: ____________________

Daily "to-do's": *shopping/errands/home tasks/etc*

____________________

____________________

Memorable Headlines or Event of the Day: *(current event from the news or in my own life)*

____________________

____________________

**Baby Countdown: 38 weeks to go**

Due Date: ____________________

Week Two Date: ____________

## Daily Encouragement

*Our devotion to God is strengthened when we offer Him a fresh commitment each day.*

Elizabeth George

Appointments today: *Doctors/Dentist/Hair/Nails/etc.*

What I'm feeling in my heart and spirit:

What I'm feeling physically:

What I ate today:

What I weighed today: ____________

Daily "to-do's": *shopping/errands/home tasks/etc*

Memorable Headlines or Event of the Day: *(current event from the news or in my own life)*

**Baby Countdown: 38 weeks to go**

Due Date: ____________

WEEK TWO Date: ____________

## DAILY ENCOURAGEMENT

*Be silent before the Lord and wait expectantly for Him.*

PSALM 37:7 HCSB

Appointments today: *Doctors/Dentist/Hair/Nails/etc.*

____________

____________

What I'm feeling in my heart and spirit:

____________

____________

What I'm feeling physically:

____________

____________

What I ate today:

____________

____________

What I weighed today: ____________

Daily "to-do's": *shopping/errands/home tasks/etc*

____________

____________

Memorable Headlines or Event of the Day: *(current event from the news or in my own life)*

____________

____________

**Baby Countdown: 38 weeks to go**

Due Date: ____________

Week Two Date: ______________________

## Daily Encouragement

*The remedy for distractions is the same now as it was in earlier and simpler times: prayer, meditation, and the cultivation of the inner life.*

A. W. Tozer

Appointments today: *Doctors/Dentist/Hair/Nails/etc.*

______________________

______________________

What I'm feeling in my heart and spirit:

______________________

______________________

What I'm feeling physically:

______________________

______________________

What I ate today:

______________________

______________________

What I weighed today: ______________________

Daily "to-do's": *shopping/errands/home tasks/etc*

______________________

______________________

Memorable Headlines or Event of the Day: *(current event from the news or in my own life)*

______________________

______________________

**Baby Countdown: 38 weeks to go**

Due Date: ______________________

## Personal Journal

You know my heart Lord…

## A Mother's Prayer:

Precious baby, I pray for you, I care for you, I love you…

Week Three Date: ____________________

## Daily Encouragement

*I leave you peace; my peace I give you. I do not give it to you as the world does. So don't let your hearts be troubled or afraid.*

JOHN 14:27 NCV

Appointments today: *Doctors/Dentist/Hair/Nails/etc.*

What I'm feeling in my heart and spirit:

What I'm feeling physically:

What I ate today:

What I weighed today: ____________________

Daily "to-do's": *shopping/errands/home tasks/etc*

Memorable Headlines or Event of the Day: *(current event from the news or in my own life)*

**Baby Countdown: 37 weeks to go**

Due Date: ____________________

WEEK THREE Date: ____________________

## DAILY ENCOURAGEMENT

*Don't be overwhelmed. Take it one day and one prayer at a time.*

STORMIE OMARTIAN

Appointments today: *Doctors/Dentist/Hair/Nails/etc.*

What I'm feeling in my heart and spirit:

What I'm feeling physically:

What I ate today:

What I weighed today: ____________________

Daily "to-do's": *shopping/errands/home tasks/etc*

Memorable Headlines or Event of the Day: *(current event from the news or in my own life)*

**Baby Countdown: 37 weeks to go**

Due Date: ____________________

WEEK THREE

Date: ______________________________

## DAILY ENCOURAGEMENT

*He Himself is our peace.*

EPHESIANS 2:14 NASB

Appointments today: *Doctors/Dentist/Hair/Nails/etc.*

What I'm feeling in my heart and spirit:

What I'm feeling physically:

What I ate today:

What I weighed today: ______________________________

Daily "to-do's": *shopping/errands/home tasks/etc*

Memorable Headlines or Event of the Day: *(current event from the news or in my own life)*

**Baby Countdown: 37 weeks to go**

Due Date: ______________________

WEEK THREE Date: ____________________

## DAILY ENCOURAGEMENT

*How changed our lives would be if we could only fly through the days on wings of surrender and trust!*

HANNAH WHITALL SMITH

Appointments today: *Doctors/Dentist/Hair/Nails/etc.*

_______________________________________________

_______________________________________________

What I'm feeling in my heart and spirit:

_______________________________________________

_______________________________________________

What I'm feeling physically:

_______________________________________________

_______________________________________________

What I ate today:

_______________________________________________

_______________________________________________

What I weighed today: ______________________________

Daily "to-do's": *shopping/errands/home tasks/etc*

_______________________________________________

_______________________________________________

Memorable Headlines or Event of the Day: *(current event from the news or in my own life)*

_______________________________________________

_______________________________________________

**Baby Countdown: 37 weeks to go**

Due Date: ____________________

WEEK THREE Date: ____________________

## DAILY ENCOURAGEMENT

*This hope we have as an anchor of the soul, both sure and steadfast, and which enters the Presence behind the veil.*

HEBREWS 6:19 NKJV

Appointments today: *Doctors/Dentist/Hair/Nails/etc.*

What I'm feeling in my heart and spirit:

What I'm feeling physically:

What I ate today:

What I weighed today: ____________________

Daily "to-do's": *shopping/errands/home tasks/etc*

Memorable Headlines or Event of the Day: *(current event from the news or in my own life)*

**Baby Countdown: 37 weeks to go**

Due Date: ____________________

## Personal Journal

You know my heart Lord…

## A Mother's Prayer:

Precious baby, I pray for you, I care for you, I love you…

Week Four Date: ____________________

## Daily Encouragement

*The life of faith is a daily exploration of the constant and countless ways in which God's grace and love are experienced.*

Eugene Peterson

Appointments today: *Doctors/Dentist/Hair/Nails/etc.*

What I'm feeling in my heart and spirit:

What I'm feeling physically:

What I ate today:

What I weighed today: ____________________

Daily "to-do's": *shopping/errands/home tasks/etc*

Memorable Headlines or Event of the Day: *(current event from the news or in my own life)*

**Baby Countdown: 36 weeks to go**

Due Date: ____________________

WEEK FOUR Date: ____________________

## DAILY ENCOURAGEMENT

*Be strong and courageous, all you who put your hope in the Lord.*

PSALM 31:24 HCSB

Appointments today: *Doctors/Dentist/Hair/Nails/etc.*

____________________

____________________

What I'm feeling in my heart and spirit:

____________________

____________________

What I'm feeling physically:

____________________

____________________

What I ate today:

____________________

____________________

What I weighed today: ____________________

Daily "to-do's": *shopping/errands/home tasks/etc*

____________________

____________________

Memorable Headlines or Event of the Day: *(current event from the news or in my own life)*

____________________

____________________

**Baby Countdown: 36 weeks to go**

Due Date: ____________________

Week Four Date: ____________________

## Daily Encouragement

*I have found the perfect antidote for fear. Whenever it sticks up its ugly face, I clobber it with prayer.*

DALE EVANS ROGERS

Appointments today: *Doctors/Dentist/Hair/Nails/etc.*

What I'm feeling in my heart and spirit:

What I'm feeling physically:

What I ate today:

What I weighed today: ____________________

Daily "to-do's": *shopping/errands/home tasks/etc*

Memorable Headlines or Event of the Day: *(current event from the news or in my own life)*

**Baby Countdown: 36 weeks to go**

Due Date: ____________________

WEEK FOUR Date: ____________________

## DAILY ENCOURAGEMENT

*Lord, I give myself to you; my God, I trust you.*

PSALM 25:1-2 NCV

Appointments today: *Doctors/Dentist/Hair/Nails/etc.*

What I'm feeling in my heart and spirit:

What I'm feeling physically:

What I ate today:

What I weighed today: ____________________

Daily "to-do's": *shopping/errands/home tasks/etc*

Memorable Headlines or Event of the Day: *(current event from the news or in my own life)*

**Baby Countdown: 36 weeks to go**

Due Date: ____________________

Week Four Date: ______________

## Daily Encouragement

*Trusting God completely means having faith that he knows what is best for your life. You expect him to keep his promises, help you with problems, and do the impossible when necessary.*

Rick Warren

Appointments today: *Doctors/Dentist/Hair/Nails/etc.*

______________

______________

What I'm feeling in my heart and spirit:

______________

______________

What I'm feeling physically:

______________

______________

What I ate today:

______________

______________

What I weighed today: ______________

Daily "to-do's": *shopping/errands/home tasks/etc*

______________

______________

Memorable Headlines or Event of the Day: *(current event from the news or in my own life)*

______________

______________

**Baby Countdown: 36 weeks to go**

Due Date: ______________

## *Personal Journal*

You know my heart Lord…

## *A Mother's Prayer:*

Precious baby, I pray for you, I care for you, I love you…

WEEK FIVE                                        *Date:* ______________________

## DAILY ENCOURAGEMENT

*I will lift up mine eyes unto the hills, from whence cometh my help.*

PSALM 121:1 KJV

Appointments today: *Doctors/Dentist/Hair/Nails/etc.*

______________________________________________

______________________________________________

What I'm feeling in my heart and spirit:

______________________________________________

______________________________________________

What I'm feeling physically:

______________________________________________

______________________________________________

What I ate today:

______________________________________________

______________________________________________

What I weighed today: ______________________________

Daily "to-do's": *shopping/errands/home tasks/etc*

______________________________________________

______________________________________________

Memorable Headlines or Event of the Day: *(current event from the news or in my own life)*

______________________________________________

______________________________________________

**Baby Countdown: 35 weeks to go**

Due Date: ______________________

Week Five Date: ____________________

## Daily Encouragement

*We look at our burdens and heavy loads, and we shrink from them. But, if we lift them and bind them about our hearts, they become wings, and on them we can rise and soar toward God.*

MRS. CHARLES E. COWMAN

Appointments today: *Doctors/Dentist/Hair/Nails/etc.*

What I'm feeling in my heart and spirit:

What I'm feeling physically:

What I ate today:

What I weighed today: ____________________

Daily "to-do's": *shopping/errands/home tasks/etc*

Memorable Headlines or Event of the Day: *(current event from the news or in my own life)*

**Baby Countdown: 35 weeks to go**

Due Date: ____________________

WEEK FIVE Date: ____________

## DAILY ENCOURAGEMENT

*For God has not given us a spirit of fearfulness, but one of power, love, and sound judgment.*

2 TIMOTHY 1:7 HCSB

Appointments today: *Doctors/Dentist/Hair/Nails/etc.*

What I'm feeling in my heart and spirit:

What I'm feeling physically:

What I ate today:

What I weighed today: ____________

Daily "to-do's": *shopping/errands/home tasks/etc*

Memorable Headlines or Event of the Day: *(current event from the news or in my own life)*

**Baby Countdown: 35 weeks to go**

Due Date: ____________

WEEK FIVE Date: ___________________

## DAILY ENCOURAGEMENT

*Why rely on yourself and fall? Cast yourself upon His arm.*
*Be not afraid. He will not let you slip.*

ST. AUGUSTINE

Appointments today: *Doctors/Dentist/Hair/Nails/etc.*

What I'm feeling in my heart and spirit:

What I'm feeling physically:

What I ate today:

What I weighed today: ___________________

Daily "to-do's": *shopping/errands/home tasks/etc*

Memorable Headlines or Event of the Day: *(current event from the news or in my own life)*

**Baby Countdown: 35 weeks to go**

Due Date: ___________________

Week Five Date: ____________________

## Daily Encouragement

*Be still, and know that I am God....*

PSALM 46:10 KJV

Appointments today: *Doctors/Dentist/Hair/Nails/etc.*

What I'm feeling in my heart and spirit:

What I'm feeling physically:

What I ate today:

What I weighed today: ____________________

Daily "to-do's": *shopping/errands/home tasks/etc*

Memorable Headlines or Event of the Day: *(current event from the news or in my own life)*

**Baby Countdown: 35 weeks to go**

Due Date: ____________________

## Personal Journal

You know my heart Lord…

## A Mother's Prayer:

Precious baby, I pray for you, I care for you, I love you…

Week Six Date: ____________

## Daily Encouragement

*We do not need to beg Him to bless us; He simply cannot help it.*

HANNAH WHITALL SMITH

Appointments today: *Doctors/Dentist/Hair/Nails/etc.*

What I'm feeling in my heart and spirit:

What I'm feeling physically:

What I ate today:

What I weighed today: ____________

Daily "to-do's": *shopping/errands/home tasks/etc*

Memorable Headlines or Event of the Day: *(current event from the news or in my own life)*

**Baby Countdown: 34 weeks to go**

Due Date: ____________

Week Six

Date: ______________________

## Daily Encouragement

*Those who hope in the LORD will renew their strength. They will soar on wings like eagles; they will run and not grow weary, they will walk and not be faint.*

ISAIAH 40:31 NIV

Appointments today: *Doctors/Dentist/Hair/Nails/etc.*

______________________

______________________

What I'm feeling in my heart and spirit:

______________________

______________________

What I'm feeling physically:

______________________

______________________

What I ate today:

______________________

______________________

What I weighed today: ______________________

Daily "to-do's": *shopping/errands/home tasks/etc*

______________________

______________________

Memorable Headlines or Event of the Day: *(current event from the news or in my own life)*

______________________

______________________

**Baby Countdown: 34 weeks to go**

Due Date: ______________________

Week Six Date: ____________________

## Daily Encouragement

*Never yield to gloomy anticipation. Place your hope and confidence in God. He has no record of failure.*

MRS. CHARLES E. COWMAN

Appointments today: *Doctors/Dentist/Hair/Nails/etc.*

______________________________

______________________________

What I'm feeling in my heart and spirit:

______________________________

______________________________

What I'm feeling physically:

______________________________

______________________________

What I ate today:

______________________________

______________________________

What I weighed today: ____________________

Daily "to-do's": *shopping/errands/home tasks/etc*

______________________________

______________________________

Memorable Headlines or Event of the Day: *(current event from the news or in my own life)*

______________________________

______________________________

**Baby Countdown: 34 weeks to go**

Due Date: ____________________

WEEK SIX Date: ____________________

DAILY ENCOURAGEMENT

*Your word is a lamp for my feet and a light on my path.*

PSALM 119:105 HCSB

Appointments today: *Doctors/Dentist/Hair/Nails/etc.*

What I'm feeling in my heart and spirit:

What I'm feeling physically:

What I ate today:

What I weighed today: ____________________

Daily "to-do's": *shopping/errands/home tasks/etc*

Memorable Headlines or Event of the Day: *(current event from the news or in my own life)*

**Baby Countdown: 34 weeks to go**

Due Date: ____________________

Week Six Date: ____________________

## Daily Encouragement

*Study the Bible and observe how the persons behaved and how God dealt with them. There is explicit teaching on every condition of life.*

CORRIE TEN BOOM

Appointments today: *Doctors/Dentist/Hair/Nails/etc.*

______________________________________________

______________________________________________

What I'm feeling in my heart and spirit:

______________________________________________

______________________________________________

What I'm feeling physically:

______________________________________________

______________________________________________

What I ate today:

______________________________________________

______________________________________________

What I weighed today: ____________________

Daily "to-do's": *shopping/errands/home tasks/etc*

______________________________________________

______________________________________________

Memorable Headlines or Event of the Day: *(current event from the news or in my own life)*

______________________________________________

______________________________________________

**Baby Countdown: 34 weeks to go**

Due Date: ____________________

Week Six

## *Personal Journal*

You know my heart Lord…

## *A Mother's Prayer:*

Precious baby, I pray for you, I care for you, I love you…

Week Seven

Date: ____________________

## Daily Encouragement

*Whatever you do, do everything for God's glory.*

1 CORINTHIANS 10:31 HCSB

Appointments today: *Doctors/Dentist/Hair/Nails/etc.*

What I'm feeling in my heart and spirit:

What I'm feeling physically:

What I ate today:

What I weighed today: ____________________

Daily "to-do's": *shopping/errands/home tasks/etc*

Memorable Headlines or Event of the Day: *(current event from the news or in my own life)*

**Baby Countdown: 33 weeks to go**

Due Date: ____________________

WEEK SEVEN　　　　　　　　*Date:* ______________________

## DAILY ENCOURAGEMENT

*Every day we live is a priceless gift of God, loaded with possibilities to learn something new, to gain fresh insights.*

DALE EVANS ROGERS

Appointments today: *Doctors/Dentist/Hair/Nails/etc.*

______________________

______________________

What I'm feeling in my heart and spirit:

______________________

______________________

What I'm feeling physically:

______________________

______________________

What I ate today:

______________________

______________________

What I weighed today: ______________________

Daily "to-do's": *shopping/errands/home tasks/etc*

______________________

______________________

Memorable Headlines or Event of the Day: *(current event from the news or in my own life)*

______________________

______________________

**Baby Countdown: 33 weeks to go**

Due Date: ______________________

WEEK SEVEN Date: ____________________

DAILY ENCOURAGEMENT

*Let us hold fast the confession of our hope without wavering, for He who promised is faithful.*

HEBREWS 10:23 NKJV

Appointments today: *Doctors/Dentist/Hair/Nails/etc.*

What I'm feeling in my heart and spirit:

What I'm feeling physically:

What I ate today:

What I weighed today: ____________________

Daily "to-do's": *shopping/errands/home tasks/etc*

Memorable Headlines or Event of the Day: *(current event from the news or in my own life)*

**Baby Countdown: 33 weeks to go**

Due Date: ____________________

Week Seven Date: ____________________

## Daily Encouragement

*Trust the past to God's mercy, the present to God's love, and the future to God's providence.*

St. Augustine

Appointments today: *Doctors/Dentist/Hair/Nails/etc.*

What I'm feeling in my heart and spirit:

What I'm feeling physically:

What I ate today:

What I weighed today: ____________________

Daily "to-do's": *shopping/errands/home tasks/etc*

Memorable Headlines or Event of the Day: *(current event from the news or in my own life)*

**Baby Countdown: 33 weeks to go**

Due Date: ____________________

Week Seven Date: ______________________

## Daily Encouragement

*Ask and it shall be given to you; seek and you shall find; knock and it shall be opened to you. For every one who asks receives, and he who seeks finds, and to him who knocks it shall be opened.*

MATTHEW 7:7-8 NASB

Appointments today: *Doctors/Dentist/Hair/Nails/etc.*

______________________________

______________________________

What I'm feeling in my heart and spirit:

______________________________

______________________________

What I'm feeling physically:

______________________________

______________________________

What I ate today:

______________________________

______________________________

What I weighed today: ______________________

Daily "to-do's": *shopping/errands/home tasks/etc*

______________________________

______________________________

Memorable Headlines or Event of the Day: *(current event from the news or in my own life)*

______________________________

______________________________

**Baby Countdown: 33 weeks to go**

Due Date: ______________________

## *Personal Journal*

You know my heart Lord…

## *A Mother's Prayer:*

Precious baby, I pray for you, I care for you, I love you…

WEEK EIGHT Date: ____________________

## DAILY ENCOURAGEMENT

*It is our part to seek, His to grant what we ask; our part to make a beginning, His to bring it to completion; our part to offer what we can, His to finish what we cannot.*

ST. JEROME

Appointments today: *Doctors/Dentist/Hair/Nails/etc.*

What I'm feeling in my heart and spirit:

What I'm feeling physically:

What I ate today:

What I weighed today: ____________________

Daily "to-do's": *shopping/errands/home tasks/etc*

Memorable Headlines or Event of the Day: *(current event from the news or in my own life)*

**Baby Countdown: 32 weeks to go**

Due Date: ____________________

Week Eight  Date: ____________

## Daily Encouragement

*Wait for the Lord; be courageous and let your heart be strong. Wait for the Lord.*

PSALM 27:14 HCSB

Appointments today: *Doctors/Dentist/Hair/Nails/etc.*

What I'm feeling in my heart and spirit:

What I'm feeling physically:

What I ate today:

What I weighed today: ____________

Daily "to-do's": *shopping/errands/home tasks/etc*

Memorable Headlines or Event of the Day: *(current event from the news or in my own life)*

**Baby Countdown: 32 weeks to go**

Due Date: ____________

Week Eight Date: ____________

## Daily Encouragement

*Waiting on God brings us to the journey's end quicker than our feet.*

MRS. CHARLES E. COWMAN

Appointments today: *Doctors/Dentist/Hair/Nails/etc.*

What I'm feeling in my heart and spirit:

What I'm feeling physically:

What I ate today:

What I weighed today: ____________

Daily "to-do's": *shopping/errands/home tasks/etc*

Memorable Headlines or Event of the Day: *(current event from the news or in my own life)*

**Baby Countdown: 32 weeks to go**

Due Date: ____________

WEEK EIGHT Date: ______________________

## DAILY ENCOURAGEMENT

*Rejoice in the Lord always. I will say it again: Rejoice!*

PHILIPPIANS 4:4 HCSB

Appointments today: *Doctors/Dentist/Hair/Nails/etc.*

______________________

______________________

What I'm feeling in my heart and spirit:

______________________

______________________

What I'm feeling physically:

______________________

______________________

What I ate today:

______________________

______________________

What I weighed today: ______________________

Daily "to-do's": *shopping/errands/home tasks/etc*

______________________

______________________

Memorable Headlines or Event of the Day: *(current event from the news or in my own life)*

______________________

______________________

**Baby Countdown: 32 weeks to go**

Due Date: ______________________

WEEK EIGHT Date: ____________________

## DAILY ENCOURAGEMENT

*The highest and most desirable state of the soul is to praise God in celebration for being alive.*

LUCI SWINDOL

Appointments today: *Doctors/Dentist/Hair/Nails/etc.*

____________________

____________________

What I'm feeling in my heart and spirit:

____________________

____________________

What I'm feeling physically:

____________________

____________________

What I ate today:

____________________

____________________

What I weighed today: ____________________

Daily "to-do's": *shopping/errands/home tasks/etc*

____________________

____________________

Memorable Headlines or Event of the Day: *(current event from the news or in my own life)*

____________________

____________________

**Baby Countdown: 32 weeks to go**

Due Date: ____________________

Week Eight

## *Personal Journal*

You know my heart Lord…

## *A Mother's Prayer:*

Precious baby, I pray for you, I care for you, I love you…

Week Nine Date: ____________________

## Daily Encouragement

*Give thanks to the Lord, for He is good; His faithful love endures forever.*

PSALM 106:1 HCSB

Appointments today: *Doctors/Dentist/Hair/Nails/etc.*

What I'm feeling in my heart and spirit:

What I'm feeling physically:

What I ate today:

What I weighed today: ____________________

Daily "to-do's": *shopping/errands/home tasks/etc*

Memorable Headlines or Event of the Day: *(current event from the news or in my own life)*

**Baby Countdown: 31 weeks to go**

Due Date: ____________________

## Week Nine

*Date:* ______________________

### Daily Encouragement

*It is only with gratitude that life becomes rich.*

DIETRICH BONHOEFFER

Appointments today: *Doctors/Dentist/Hair/Nails/etc.*

______________________

______________________

What I'm feeling in my heart and spirit:

______________________

______________________

What I'm feeling physically:

______________________

______________________

What I ate today:

______________________

______________________

What I weighed today: ______________________

Daily "to-do's": *shopping/errands/home tasks/etc*

______________________

______________________

Memorable Headlines or Event of the Day: *(current event from the news or in my own life)*

______________________

______________________

**Baby Countdown: 31 weeks to go**

Due Date: ______________________

Week Nine Date: ______________________

## Daily Encouragement

*Keep your eyes focused on what is right, and look straight ahead to what is good.*

PROVERBS 4:25 NCV

Appointments today: *Doctors/Dentist/Hair/Nails/etc.*

___

___

What I'm feeling in my heart and spirit:

___

___

What I'm feeling physically:

___

___

What I ate today:

___

___

What I weighed today: ______________________

Daily "to-do's": *shopping/errands/home tasks/etc*

___

___

Memorable Headlines or Event of the Day: *(current event from the news or in my own life)*

___

___

**Baby Countdown: 31 weeks to go**

Due Date: ______________________

WEEK NINE

*Date:* ______________________

## DAILY ENCOURAGEMENT

*Developing a positive attitude means working continually to find what is uplifting and encouraging.*

BARBARA JOHNSON

Appointments today: *Doctors/Dentist/Hair/Nails/etc.*

______________________

______________________

What I'm feeling in my heart and spirit:

______________________

______________________

What I'm feeling physically:

______________________

______________________

What I ate today:

______________________

______________________

What I weighed today: ______________________

Daily "to-do's": *shopping/errands/home tasks/etc*

______________________

______________________

Memorable Headlines or Event of the Day: *(current event from the news or in my own life)*

______________________

______________________

**Baby Countdown: 31 weeks to go**

Due Date: ______________________

WEEK NINE Date: ____________________

## DAILY ENCOURAGEMENT

*He gives power to the weak, and to those who have no might He increases strength.*

ISAIAH 40:29 NKJV

Appointments today: *Doctors/Dentist/Hair/Nails/etc.*

______________________________

______________________________

What I'm feeling in my heart and spirit:

______________________________

______________________________

What I'm feeling physically:

______________________________

______________________________

What I ate today:

______________________________

______________________________

What I weighed today: ____________________

Daily "to-do's": *shopping/errands/home tasks/etc*

______________________________

______________________________

Memorable Headlines or Event of the Day: *(current event from the news or in my own life)*

______________________________

______________________________

**Baby Countdown: 31 weeks to go**

Due Date: ____________________

## Personal Journal

You know my heart Lord…

## A Mother's Prayer:

Precious baby, I pray for you, I care for you, I love you…

Week Ten Date: ______________________

## Daily Encouragement

*The mind is like a clock that is constantly running down. It has to be wound up daily with good thoughts.*

FULTON J. SHEEN

Appointments today: *Doctors/Dentist/Hair/Nails/etc.*

______________________

______________________

What I'm feeling in my heart and spirit:

______________________

______________________

What I'm feeling physically:

______________________

______________________

What I ate today:

______________________

______________________

What I weighed today: ______________________

Daily "to-do's": *shopping/errands/home tasks/etc*

______________________

______________________

Memorable Headlines or Event of the Day: *(current event from the news or in my own life)*

______________________

______________________

**Baby Countdown: 30 weeks to go**

Due Date: ______________________

WEEK TEN Date: ____________________

## DAILY ENCOURAGEMENT

*Rejoice in hope; be patient in affliction; be persistent in prayer.*

ROMANS 12:12 HCSB

Appointments today: *Doctors/Dentist/Hair/Nails/etc.*

______________________________

______________________________

What I'm feeling in my heart and spirit:

______________________________

______________________________

What I'm feeling physically:

______________________________

______________________________

What I ate today:

______________________________

______________________________

What I weighed today: ____________________

Daily "to-do's": *shopping/errands/home tasks/etc*

______________________________

______________________________

Memorable Headlines or Event of the Day: *(current event from the news or in my own life)*

______________________________

______________________________

**Baby Countdown: 30 weeks to go**

Due Date: ____________________

WEEK TEN Date: ____________

## DAILY ENCOURAGEMENT

*No matter what we are going through, no matter how long the waiting for answers, of one thing we may be sure. God is faithful. He keeps His promises. What he starts, He finishes, including His perfect work in us.*

GLORIA GAITHER

Appointments today: *Doctors/Dentist/Hair/Nails/etc.*

---

---

What I'm feeling in my heart and spirit:

---

---

What I'm feeling physically:

---

---

What I ate today:

---

---

What I weighed today: ____________

Daily "to-do's": *shopping/errands/home tasks/etc*

---

---

Memorable Headlines or Event of the Day: *(current event from the news or in my own life)*

---

---

**Baby Countdown: 30 weeks to go**

Due Date: ____________

Date: ____________________

## Daily Encouragement

*And do not be conformed to this world, but be transformed by the renewing of your mind, that you may prove what is that good and acceptable and perfect will of God.*

ROMANS 12:2 NKJV

Appointments today: *Doctors/Dentist/Hair/Nails/etc.*

What I'm feeling in my heart and spirit:

What I'm feeling physically:

What I ate today:

What I weighed today: ____________________

Daily "to-do's": *shopping/errands/home tasks/etc*

Memorable Headlines or Event of the Day: *(current event from the news or in my own life)*

**Baby Countdown: 30 weeks to go**

Due Date: ____________________

WEEK TEN Date: ______________

## DAILY ENCOURAGEMENT

*For God is, indeed, a wonderful Father who longs to pour out His mercy upon us, and whose majesty is so great that He can transform us from deep within.*

ST. TERESA OF AVILA

Appointments today: *Doctors/Dentist/Hair/Nails/etc.*

______________

______________

What I'm feeling in my heart and spirit:

______________

______________

What I'm feeling physically:

______________

______________

What I ate today:

______________

______________

What I weighed today: ______________

Daily "to-do's": *shopping/errands/home tasks/etc*

______________

______________

Memorable Headlines or Event of the Day: *(current event from the news or in my own life)*

______________

______________

**Baby Countdown: 30 weeks to go**

Due Date: ______________

## Personal Journal

You know my heart Lord...

## A Mother's Prayer:

Precious baby, I pray for you, I care for you, I love you...

Date: ____________________

## DAILY ENCOURAGEMENT

*These things have I spoken unto you, that my joy might remain in you, and that your joy might be full.*

JOHN 15:11 KJV

Appointments today: *Doctors/Dentist/Hair/Nails/etc.*

______________________________

______________________________

What I'm feeling in my heart and spirit:

______________________________

______________________________

What I'm feeling physically:

______________________________

______________________________

What I ate today:

______________________________

______________________________

What I weighed today: ____________________

Daily "to-do's": *shopping/errands/home tasks/etc*

______________________________

______________________________

Memorable Headlines or Event of the Day: *(current event from the news or in my own life)*

______________________________

______________________________

**Baby Countdown: 29 weeks to go**

Due Date: ____________________

Week Eleven Date: ____________________

## Daily Encouragement

*God is the giver, and we are the receivers. And His richest gifts are bestowed not upon those who do the greatest things, but upon those who accept His abundance and His grace.*

HANNAH WHITALL SMITH

Appointments today: *Doctors/Dentist/Hair/Nails/etc.*

What I'm feeling in my heart and spirit:

What I'm feeling physically:

What I ate today:

What I weighed today: ____________________

Daily "to-do's": *shopping/errands/home tasks/etc*

Memorable Headlines or Event of the Day: *(current event from the news or in my own life)*

**Baby Countdown: 29 weeks to go**

Due Date: ____________________

Week Eleven Date: ______________________

## Daily Encouragement

*The Lord bless you and keep you; The Lord make His face shine upon you,*
*And be gracious to you.*

NUMBERS 6:24-25 NKJV

Appointments today: *Doctors/Dentist/Hair/Nails/etc.*

_______________________________________________

_______________________________________________

What I'm feeling in my heart and spirit:

_______________________________________________

_______________________________________________

What I'm feeling physically:

_______________________________________________

_______________________________________________

What I ate today:

_______________________________________________

_______________________________________________

What I weighed today: ______________________

Daily "to-do's": *shopping/errands/home tasks/etc*

_______________________________________________

_______________________________________________

Memorable Headlines or Event of the Day: *(current event from the news or in my own life)*

_______________________________________________

_______________________________________________

**Baby Countdown: 29 weeks to go**

Due Date: ______________________

Week Eleven Date: ____________________

## Daily Encouragement

*Do we not continually pass by blessings innumerable without notice, and instead fix our eyes on what we feel to be our trials and our losses, and think and talk about these until our whole horizon is filled with them, and we almost begin to think we have no blessings at all?*

HANNAH WHITALL SMITH

Appointments today: *Doctors/Dentist/Hair/Nails/etc.*

____________________

____________________

What I'm feeling in my heart and spirit:

____________________

____________________

What I'm feeling physically:

____________________

____________________

What I ate today:

____________________

____________________

What I weighed today: ____________________

Daily "to-do's": *shopping/errands/home tasks/etc*

____________________

____________________

Memorable Headlines or Event of the Day: *(current event from the news or in my own life)*

____________________

____________________

**Baby Countdown: 29 weeks to go**

Due Date: ____________________

Week Eleven Date: ______________________

## Daily Encouragement

*Without wavering, let us hold tightly to the hope we say we have, for God can be trusted to keep his promise.*

HEBREWS 10:23 NLT

Appointments today: *Doctors/Dentist/Hair/Nails/etc.*

______________________

______________________

What I'm feeling in my heart and spirit:

______________________

______________________

What I'm feeling physically:

______________________

______________________

What I ate today:

______________________

______________________

What I weighed today: ______________________

Daily "to-do's": *shopping/errands/home tasks/etc*

______________________

______________________

Memorable Headlines or Event of the Day: *(current event from the news or in my own life)*

______________________

______________________

**Baby Countdown: 29 weeks to go**

Due Date: ______________________

Week Eleven

## *Personal Journal*

You know my heart Lord…

## *A Mother's Prayer:*

Precious baby, I pray for you, I care for you, I love you…

WEEK TWELVE Date: ______________________

## DAILY ENCOURAGEMENT

*Fear and doubt are conquered by a faith that rejoices. And faith can rejoice because the promises of God are as certain as God Himself.*

KAY ARTHUR

Appointments today: *Doctors/Dentist/Hair/Nails/etc.*

______________________________________________

______________________________________________

What I'm feeling in my heart and spirit:

______________________________________________

______________________________________________

What I'm feeling physically:

______________________________________________

______________________________________________

What I ate today:

______________________________________________

______________________________________________

What I weighed today: ______________________________

Daily "to-do's": *shopping/errands/home tasks/etc*

______________________________________________

______________________________________________

Memorable Headlines or Event of the Day: *(current event from the news or in my own life)*

______________________________________________

______________________________________________

**Baby Countdown: 28 weeks to go**

Due Date: ______________________

WEEK TWELVE Date: ______________________

## DAILY ENCOURAGEMENT

*I wait for the Lord, my soul waits, And in His word I do hope.*
*My soul waits for the Lord More than those who watch for the morning—*
*Yes, more than those who watch for the morning.*

PSALM 130:5-6 NKJV

Appointments today: *Doctors/Dentist/Hair/Nails/etc.*

______________________

______________________

What I'm feeling in my heart and spirit:

______________________

______________________

What I'm feeling physically:

______________________

______________________

What I ate today:

______________________

______________________

What I weighed today: ______________________

Daily "to-do's": *shopping/errands/home tasks/etc*

______________________

______________________

Memorable Headlines or Event of the Day: *(current event from the news or in my own life)*

______________________

______________________

**Baby Countdown: 28 weeks to go**

Due Date: ______________________

WEEK TWELVE Date: ______________

## DAILY ENCOURAGEMENT

*All things pass. Patience attains all it strives for.*

ST. TERESA OF AVILA

Appointments today: *Doctors/Dentist/Hair/Nails/etc.*

______________

______________

What I'm feeling in my heart and spirit:

______________

______________

What I'm feeling physically:

______________

______________

What I ate today:

______________

______________

What I weighed today: ______________

Daily "to-do's": *shopping/errands/home tasks/etc*

______________

______________

Memorable Headlines or Event of the Day: *(current event from the news or in my own life)*

______________

______________

**Baby Countdown: 28 weeks to go**

Due Date: ______________

WEEK TWELVE Date: ____________________

## DAILY ENCOURAGEMENT

*For you have need of endurance, so that when you have done the will of God, you may receive what was promised.*

HEBREWS 10:36 NASB

Appointments today: *Doctors/Dentist/Hair/Nails/etc.*

What I'm feeling in my heart and spirit:

What I'm feeling physically:

What I ate today:

What I weighed today: ____________________

Daily "to-do's": *shopping/errands/home tasks/etc*

Memorable Headlines or Event of the Day: *(current event from the news or in my own life)*

**Baby Countdown: 28 weeks to go**

Due Date: ____________________

WEEK TWELVE Date: ____________________

## DAILY ENCOURAGEMENT

*Whether our fear is absolutely realistic or out of proportion in our minds, our greatest refuge is Jesus Christ.*

LUCI SWINDOLL

Appointments today: *Doctors/Dentist/Hair/Nails/etc.*

______________________________________________

______________________________________________

What I'm feeling in my heart and spirit:

______________________________________________

______________________________________________

What I'm feeling physically:

______________________________________________

______________________________________________

What I ate today:

______________________________________________

______________________________________________

What I weighed today: ____________________

Daily "to-do's": *shopping/errands/home tasks/etc*

______________________________________________

______________________________________________

Memorable Headlines or Event of the Day: *(current event from the news or in my own life)*

______________________________________________

______________________________________________

**Baby Countdown: 28 weeks to go**

Due Date: ____________________

Week Twelve

## *Personal Journal*

You know my heart Lord...

## *A Mother's Prayer:*

Precious baby, I pray for you, I care for you, I love you...

Week Thirteen Date: ______________________

## Daily Encouragement

*And whatever you do, in word or in deed, do everything in the name of the Lord Jesus, giving thanks to God the Father through Him.*

COLOSSIANS 3:17 HCSB

Appointments today: *Doctors/Dentist/Hair/Nails/etc.*

What I'm feeling in my heart and spirit:

What I'm feeling physically:

What I ate today:

What I weighed today: ______________________

Daily "to-do's": *shopping/errands/home tasks/etc*

Memorable Headlines or Event of the Day: *(current event from the news or in my own life)*

**Baby Countdown: 27 weeks to go**

Due Date: ______________________

WEEK THIRTEEN Date: ______________

## DAILY ENCOURAGEMENT

*God is in control, and therefore in everything I can give thanks, not because of the situation, but because of the One who directs and rules over it.*

KAY ARTHUR

Appointments today: *Doctors/Dentist/Hair/Nails/etc.*

______________

______________

What I'm feeling in my heart and spirit:

______________

______________

What I'm feeling physically:

______________

______________

What I ate today:

______________

______________

What I weighed today: ______________

Daily "to-do's": *shopping/errands/home tasks/etc*

______________

______________

Memorable Headlines or Event of the Day: *(current event from the news or in my own life)*

______________

______________

**Baby Countdown: 27 weeks to go**

Due Date: ______________

Week Thirteen Date: ____________________

## Daily Encouragement

*One thing I do, forgetting those things which are behind and reaching forward to those things which are ahead, I press toward the goal for the prize of the upward call of God in Christ Jesus.*

PHILIPPIANS 3:13-14 NKJV

Appointments today: *Doctors/Dentist/Hair/Nails/etc.*

___________________________________________

___________________________________________

What I'm feeling in my heart and spirit:

___________________________________________

___________________________________________

What I'm feeling physically:

___________________________________________

___________________________________________

What I ate today:

___________________________________________

___________________________________________

What I weighed today: ____________________

Daily "to-do's": *shopping/errands/home tasks/etc*

___________________________________________

___________________________________________

Memorable Headlines or Event of the Day: *(current event from the news or in my own life)*

___________________________________________

___________________________________________

**Baby Countdown: 27 weeks to go**

Due Date: ____________________

WEEK THIRTEEN Date: ____________________

## DAILY ENCOURAGEMENT

*We need to be at peace with our past, content with our present, and sure about our future, knowing they are all in God's hands.*

JOYCE MEYER

Appointments today: *Doctors/Dentist/Hair/Nails/etc.*

What I'm feeling in my heart and spirit:

What I'm feeling physically:

What I ate today:

What I weighed today: ____________________

Daily "to-do's": *shopping/errands/home tasks/etc*

Memorable Headlines or Event of the Day: *(current event from the news or in my own life)*

**Baby Countdown: 27 weeks to go**

Due Date: ____________________

Week Thirteen Date: ____________

## Daily Encouragement

*Depend on the Lord and his strength; always go to him for help. Remember the miracles he has done; remember his wonders and his decisions.*

PSALM 105:4-5 NCV

Appointments today: *Doctors/Dentist/Hair/Nails/etc.*

What I'm feeling in my heart and spirit:

What I'm feeling physically:

What I ate today:

What I weighed today: ____________

Daily "to-do's": *shopping/errands/home tasks/etc*

Memorable Headlines or Event of the Day: *(current event from the news or in my own life)*

**Baby Countdown: 27 weeks to go**

Due Date: ____________

## Personal Journal

You know my heart Lord…

## A Mother's Prayer:

Precious baby, I pray for you, I care for you, I love you…

Week Fourteen Date: ____________________

## Daily Encouragement

*Remember always that there are two things which are more utterly incompatible even than oil and water, and these two are trust and worry.*

HANNAH WHITALL SMITH

Appointments today: *Doctors/Dentist/Hair/Nails/etc.*

______________________________

______________________________

What I'm feeling in my heart and spirit:

______________________________

______________________________

What I'm feeling physically:

______________________________

______________________________

What I ate today:

______________________________

______________________________

What I weighed today: ____________________

Daily "to-do's": *shopping/errands/home tasks/etc*

______________________________

______________________________

Memorable Headlines or Event of the Day: *(current event from the news or in my own life)*

______________________________

______________________________

**Baby Countdown: 26 weeks to go**

Due Date: ____________________

WEEK FOURTEEN Date: ____________

## DAILY ENCOURAGEMENT

*Therefore don't worry about tomorrow, because tomorrow will worry about itself. Each day has enough trouble of its own.*

MATTHEW 6:34 HCSB

Appointments today: *Doctors/Dentist/Hair/Nails/etc.*

What I'm feeling in my heart and spirit:

What I'm feeling physically:

What I ate today:

What I weighed today: ____________

Daily "to-do's": *shopping/errands/home tasks/etc*

Memorable Headlines or Event of the Day: *(current event from the news or in my own life)*

**Baby Countdown: 26 weeks to go**

Due Date: ____________

Week Fourteen Date: ____________

## Daily Encouragement

*Put your hand into the hand of God. He gives the calmness and serenity of heart and soul.*

Mrs. Charles E. Cowman

Appointments today: *Doctors/Dentist/Hair/Nails/etc.*

What I'm feeling in my heart and spirit:

What I'm feeling physically:

What I ate today:

What I weighed today: ____________

Daily "to-do's": *shopping/errands/home tasks/etc*

Memorable Headlines or Event of the Day: *(current event from the news or in my own life)*

**Baby Countdown: 26 weeks to go**

Due Date: ____________

WEEK FOURTEEN     *Date:* ______________________

## DAILY ENCOURAGEMENT

*I wait quietly before God, for my hope is in him.*

PSALM 62:5 NLT

Appointments today: *Doctors/Dentist/Hair/Nails/etc.*

______________________

______________________

What I'm feeling in my heart and spirit:

______________________

______________________

What I'm feeling physically:

______________________

______________________

What I ate today:

______________________

______________________

What I weighed today: ______________________

Daily "to-do's": *shopping/errands/home tasks/etc*

______________________

______________________

Memorable Headlines or Event of the Day: *(current event from the news or in my own life)*

______________________

______________________

**Baby Countdown: 26 weeks to go**

Due Date: ______________________

Week Fourteen Date: ____________________

## Daily Encouragement

*When you live a surrendered life, God is willing and able to provide for your every need.*

CORRIE TEN BOOM

Appointments today: *Doctors/Dentist/Hair/Nails/etc.*

____________________

____________________

What I'm feeling in my heart and spirit:

____________________

____________________

What I'm feeling physically:

____________________

____________________

What I ate today:

____________________

____________________

What I weighed today: ____________________

Daily "to-do's": *shopping/errands/home tasks/etc*

____________________

____________________

Memorable Headlines or Event of the Day: *(current event from the news or in my own life)*

____________________

____________________

**Baby Countdown: 26 weeks to go**

Due Date: ____________________

WEEK FOURTEEN

## Personal Journal

YOU KNOW MY HEART LORD…

## A Mother's Prayer:

PRECIOUS BABY, I PRAY FOR YOU, I CARE FOR YOU, I LOVE YOU…

Week Fifteen Date: ____________________

## Daily Encouragement

*One Lord, one faith, one baptism, one God and Father of all, who is above all and through all and in all.*

Ephesians 4:5-6 HCSB

Appointments today: *Doctors/Dentist/Hair/Nails/etc.*

What I'm feeling in my heart and spirit:

What I'm feeling physically:

What I ate today:

What I weighed today: ____________________

Daily "to-do's": *shopping/errands/home tasks/etc*

Memorable Headlines or Event of the Day: *(current event from the news or in my own life)*

**Baby Countdown: 25 weeks to go**

Due Date: ____________________

Week Fifteen Date: ______________________

## Daily Encouragement

*Let nothing disturb you, nothing frighten you; all things are passing;
God never changes.*

ST. TERESA OF AVILA

Appointments today: *Doctors/Dentist/Hair/Nails/etc.*

______________________

______________________

What I'm feeling in my heart and spirit:

______________________

______________________

What I'm feeling physically:

______________________

______________________

What I ate today:

______________________

______________________

What I weighed today: ______________________

Daily "to-do's": *shopping/errands/home tasks/etc*

______________________

______________________

Memorable Headlines or Event of the Day: *(current event from the news or in my own life)*

______________________

______________________

**Baby Countdown: 25 weeks to go**

Due Date: ______________________

Week Fifteen Date: ______________________

## Daily Encouragement

*But as it is written in the Scriptures: "No one has ever seen this, and no one has ever heard about it. No one has ever imagined what God has prepared for those who love him."*

1 CORINTHIANS 2:9 NCV

Appointments today: *Doctors/Dentist/Hair/Nails/etc.*

______________________________________________

______________________________________________

What I'm feeling in my heart and spirit:

______________________________________________

______________________________________________

What I'm feeling physically:

______________________________________________

______________________________________________

What I ate today:

______________________________________________

______________________________________________

What I weighed today: ______________________________

Daily "to-do's": *shopping/errands/home tasks/etc*

______________________________________________

______________________________________________

Memorable Headlines or Event of the Day: *(current event from the news or in my own life)*

______________________________________________

______________________________________________

**Baby Countdown: 25 weeks to go**

Due Date: ______________________

Week Fifteen — Date: ____________________

## Daily Encouragement

*Only believe, don't fear. Our Master, Jesus, always watches over us, and no matter what the persecution, Jesus will surely overcome it.*

LOTTIE MOON

Appointments today: *Doctors/Dentist/Hair/Nails/etc.*

____________________

____________________

What I'm feeling in my heart and spirit:

____________________

____________________

What I'm feeling physically:

____________________

____________________

What I ate today:

____________________

____________________

What I weighed today: ____________________

Daily "to-do's": *shopping/errands/home tasks/etc*

____________________

____________________

Memorable Headlines or Event of the Day: *(current event from the news or in my own life)*

____________________

____________________

**Baby Countdown: 25 weeks to go**

Due Date: ____________________

Week Fifteen Date: ______________________

## Daily Encouragement

*Our help is in the name of the Lord, the Maker of heaven and earth.*

PSALM 124:8 HCSB

Appointments today: *Doctors/Dentist/Hair/Nails/etc.*

______________________

______________________

What I'm feeling in my heart and spirit:

______________________

______________________

What I'm feeling physically:

______________________

______________________

What I ate today:

______________________

______________________

What I weighed today: ______________________

Daily "to-do's": *shopping/errands/home tasks/etc*

______________________

______________________

Memorable Headlines or Event of the Day: *(current event from the news or in my own life)*

______________________

______________________

**Baby Countdown: 25 weeks to go**

Due Date: ______________________

## Week Fifteen

You know my heart Lord…

Precious baby, I pray for you, I care for you, I love you…

## Week Sixteen

*Date:* ____________________

### Daily Encouragement

*When once we are assured that God is good, then there can be nothing left to fear.*

HANNAH WHITALL SMITH

Appointments today: *Doctors/Dentist/Hair/Nails/etc.*

What I'm feeling in my heart and spirit:

What I'm feeling physically:

What I ate today:

What I weighed today: ____________________

Daily "to-do's": *shopping/errands/home tasks/etc*

Memorable Headlines or Event of the Day: *(current event from the news or in my own life)*

**Baby Countdown: 24 weeks to go**

Due Date: ____________________

WEEK SIXTEEN Date: ______________________

## DAILY ENCOURAGEMENT

*Therefore humble yourselves under the mighty hand of God, that He may exalt you at the proper time, casting all your anxiety on Him, because He cares for you.*

1 PETER 5:6-7 NASB

Appointments today: *Doctors/Dentist/Hair/Nails/etc.*

______________________________________________

______________________________________________

What I'm feeling in my heart and spirit:

______________________________________________

______________________________________________

What I'm feeling physically:

______________________________________________

______________________________________________

What I ate today:

______________________________________________

______________________________________________

What I weighed today: ______________________________

Daily "to-do's": *shopping/errands/home tasks/etc*

______________________________________________

______________________________________________

Memorable Headlines or Event of the Day: *(current event from the news or in my own life)*

______________________________________________

______________________________________________

**Baby Countdown: 24 weeks to go**

Due Date: ______________________

WEEK SIXTEEN  *Date:* ____________________

## DAILY ENCOURAGEMENT

*The unfolding of our friendship with the Father will be a never-ending revelation stretching on into eternity.*

CATHERINE MARSHALL

Appointments today: *Doctors/Dentist/Hair/Nails/etc.*

____________________

____________________

What I'm feeling in my heart and spirit:

____________________

____________________

What I'm feeling physically:

____________________

____________________

What I ate today:

____________________

____________________

What I weighed today: ____________________

Daily "to-do's": *shopping/errands/home tasks/etc*

____________________

____________________

Memorable Headlines or Event of the Day: *(current event from the news or in my own life)*

____________________

____________________

**Baby Countdown: 24 weeks to go**

Due Date: ____________________

Week Sixteen

*Date:* ______________________

## Daily Encouragement

*So do not fear, for I am with you; do not be dismayed, for I am your God. I will strengthen you and help you; I will uphold you with my righteous right hand.*

ISAIAH 41:10 NIV

Appointments today: *Doctors/Dentist/Hair/Nails/etc.*

What I'm feeling in my heart and spirit:

What I'm feeling physically:

What I ate today:

What I weighed today: ______________________

Daily "to-do's": *shopping/errands/home tasks/etc*

Memorable Headlines or Event of the Day: *(current event from the news or in my own life)*

**Baby Countdown: 24 weeks to go**

Due Date: ______________________

WEEK SIXTEEN Date: ____________________

## DAILY ENCOURAGEMENT

*If God has you in the palm of his hand and your real life is secure in him, then you can venture forth— into the places and relationships, the challenges, the very heart of the storm—and you will be safe there.*

PAULA RINEHART

Appointments today: *Doctors/Dentist/Hair/Nails/etc.*

What I'm feeling in my heart and spirit:

What I'm feeling physically:

What I ate today:

What I weighed today: ____________________

Daily "to-do's": *shopping/errands/home tasks/etc*

Memorable Headlines or Event of the Day: *(current event from the news or in my own life)*

**Baby Countdown: 24 weeks to go**

Due Date: ____________________

## Personal Journal

You know my heart Lord…

## A Mother's Prayer:

Precious baby, I pray for you, I care for you, I love you…

WEEK SEVENTEEN Date: ____________________

## DAILY ENCOURAGEMENT

*We know that all things work together for the good of those who love God: those who are called according to His purpose.*

ROMANS 8:28 HCSB

Appointments today: *Doctors/Dentist/Hair/Nails/etc.*

---

---

What I'm feeling in my heart and spirit:

---

---

What I'm feeling physically:

---

---

What I ate today:

---

---

What I weighed today: ____________________

Daily "to-do's": *shopping/errands/home tasks/etc*

---

---

Memorable Headlines or Event of the Day: *(current event from the news or in my own life)*

---

---

**Baby Countdown: 23 weeks to go**

Due Date: ____________________

Week Seventeen Date: ____________________

## Daily Encouragement

*If you believe in a God who controls the big things, you have to believe in a God who controls the little things. It is we, of course, to whom things look "little" or "big."*

ELISABETH ELLIOT

Appointments today: *Doctors/Dentist/Hair/Nails/etc.*

What I'm feeling in my heart and spirit:

What I'm feeling physically:

What I ate today:

What I weighed today: ____________________

Daily "to-do's": *shopping/errands/home tasks/etc*

Memorable Headlines or Event of the Day: *(current event from the news or in my own life)*

**Baby Countdown: 23 weeks to go**

Due Date: ____________________

Week Seventeen Date: ______________________

## Daily Encouragement

*How happy is everyone who fears the Lord, who walks in His ways!*

PSALM 128:1 HCSB

Appointments today: *Doctors/Dentist/Hair/Nails/etc.*

______________________

______________________

What I'm feeling in my heart and spirit:

______________________

______________________

What I'm feeling physically:

______________________

______________________

What I ate today:

______________________

______________________

What I weighed today: ______________________

Daily "to-do's": *shopping/errands/home tasks/etc*

______________________

______________________

Memorable Headlines or Event of the Day: *(current event from the news or in my own life)*

______________________

______________________

**Baby Countdown: 23 weeks to go**

Due Date: ______________________

Week Seventeen Date: ____________________

## Daily Encouragement

*The Reference Point for the Christian is the Bible. All values, judgments, and attitudes must be gauged in relationship to this Reference Point.*

RUTH BELL GRAHAM

Appointments today: *Doctors/Dentist/Hair/Nails/etc.*

______________________________

______________________________

What I'm feeling in my heart and spirit:

______________________________

______________________________

What I'm feeling physically:

______________________________

______________________________

What I ate today:

______________________________

______________________________

What I weighed today: ____________________

Daily "to-do's": *shopping/errands/home tasks/etc*

______________________________

______________________________

Memorable Headlines or Event of the Day: *(current event from the news or in my own life)*

______________________________

______________________________

**Baby Countdown: 23 weeks to go**

Due Date: ____________________

WEEK SEVENTEEN Date: ______________________

DAILY ENCOURAGEMENT

*You will show me the way of life, granting me the joy of your presence and the pleasures of living with you forever.*

PSALM 16:11 NLT

Appointments today: *Doctors/Dentist/Hair/Nails/etc.*

______________________________

______________________________

What I'm feeling in my heart and spirit:

______________________________

______________________________

What I'm feeling physically:

______________________________

______________________________

What I ate today:

______________________________

______________________________

What I weighed today: ______________________

Daily "to-do's": *shopping/errands/home tasks/etc*

______________________________

______________________________

Memorable Headlines or Event of the Day: *(current event from the news or in my own life)*

______________________________

______________________________

**Baby Countdown: 23 weeks to go**

Due Date: ______________________

## Personal Journal

YOU KNOW MY HEART LORD...

## A Mother's Prayer:

PRECIOUS BABY, I PRAY FOR YOU, I CARE FOR YOU, I LOVE YOU...

WEEK EIGHTEEN Date: ____________

DAILY ENCOURAGEMENT

*Joy is the serious business of heaven.*

C. S. LEWIS

Appointments today: *Doctors/Dentist/Hair/Nails/etc.*

What I'm feeling in my heart and spirit:

What I'm feeling physically:

What I ate today:

What I weighed today: ____________

Daily "to-do's": *shopping/errands/home tasks/etc*

Memorable Headlines or Event of the Day: *(current event from the news or in my own life)*

**Baby Countdown: 22 weeks to go**

Due Date: ____________

Week Eighteen Date: ______________________

## Daily Encouragement

*The unfailing love of the Lord never ends!*

LAMENTATIONS 3:22 NLT

Appointments today: *Doctors/Dentist/Hair/Nails/etc.*

______________________________________________

______________________________________________

What I'm feeling in my heart and spirit:

______________________________________________

______________________________________________

What I'm feeling physically:

______________________________________________

______________________________________________

What I ate today:

______________________________________________

______________________________________________

What I weighed today: ______________________________

Daily "to-do's": *shopping/errands/home tasks/etc*

______________________________________________

______________________________________________

Memorable Headlines or Event of the Day: *(current event from the news or in my own life)*

______________________________________________

______________________________________________

**Baby Countdown: 22 weeks to go**

Due Date: ______________________

WEEK EIGHTEEN Date: ____________________

## DAILY ENCOURAGEMENT

*God will never let you be shaken or moved from your place near His heart.*

JONI EARECKSON TADA

Appointments today: *Doctors/Dentist/Hair/Nails/etc.*

______________________________

______________________________

What I'm feeling in my heart and spirit:

______________________________

______________________________

What I'm feeling physically:

______________________________

______________________________

What I ate today:

______________________________

______________________________

What I weighed today: ____________________

Daily "to-do's": *shopping/errands/home tasks/etc*

______________________________

______________________________

Memorable Headlines or Event of the Day: *(current event from the news or in my own life)*

______________________________

______________________________

**Baby Countdown: 22 weeks to go**

Due Date: ____________________

WEEK EIGHTEEN  *Date:* ____________________

## DAILY ENCOURAGEMENT

*Seek the Lord, and ye shall live....*

AMOS 5:6 KJV

Appointments today: *Doctors/Dentist/Hair/Nails/etc.*

______________________________

______________________________

What I'm feeling in my heart and spirit:

______________________________

______________________________

What I'm feeling physically:

______________________________

______________________________

What I ate today:

______________________________

______________________________

What I weighed today: ____________________

Daily "to-do's": *shopping/errands/home tasks/etc*

______________________________

______________________________

Memorable Headlines or Event of the Day: *(current event from the news or in my own life)*

______________________________

______________________________

**Baby Countdown: 22 weeks to go**

Due Date: ____________________

Week Eighteen Date: ____________________

## Daily Encouragement

*You have a glorious future in Christ! Live every moment in His power and love.*

VONETTE BRIGHT

Appointments today: *Doctors/Dentist/Hair/Nails/etc.*

______________________________

______________________________

What I'm feeling in my heart and spirit:

______________________________

______________________________

What I'm feeling physically:

______________________________

______________________________

What I ate today:

______________________________

______________________________

What I weighed today: ____________________

Daily "to-do's": *shopping/errands/home tasks/etc*

______________________________

______________________________

Memorable Headlines or Event of the Day: *(current event from the news or in my own life)*

______________________________

______________________________

**Baby Countdown: 22 weeks to go**

Due Date: ____________________

Week Eighteen

## *Personal Journal*

You know my heart Lord…

## *A Mother's Prayer:*

Precious baby, I pray for you, I care for you, I love you…

Week Nineteen Date: ______________________

## Daily Encouragement

*Do not be afraid or discouraged, for the LORD is the one who goes before you. He will be with you; he will neither fail you nor forsake you.*

DEUTERONOMY 31:8 NLT

Appointments today: *Doctors/Dentist/Hair/Nails/etc.*

______________________

______________________

What I'm feeling in my heart and spirit:

______________________

______________________

What I'm feeling physically:

______________________

______________________

What I ate today:

______________________

______________________

What I weighed today: ______________________

Daily "to-do's": *shopping/errands/home tasks/etc*

______________________

______________________

Memorable Headlines or Event of the Day: *(current event from the news or in my own life)*

______________________

______________________

**Baby Countdown: 21 weeks to go**

Due Date: ______________________

WEEK NINETEEN Date: ______________________

## DAILY ENCOURAGEMENT

*Ours is an intentional God, brimming over with motive and mission. He never does things capriciously or decides with the flip of a coin.*

JONI EARECKSON TADA

Appointments today: *Doctors/Dentist/Hair/Nails/etc.*

What I'm feeling in my heart and spirit:

What I'm feeling physically:

What I ate today:

What I weighed today: ______________________

Daily "to-do's": *shopping/errands/home tasks/etc*

Memorable Headlines or Event of the Day: *(current event from the news or in my own life)*

**Baby Countdown: 21 weeks to go**

Due Date: ______________________

WEEK NINETEEN Date: ____________

DAILY ENCOURAGEMENT

*Let not your heart be troubled.*

JOHN 14:1 KJV

Appointments today: *Doctors/Dentist/Hair/Nails/etc.*

What I'm feeling in my heart and spirit:

What I'm feeling physically:

What I ate today:

What I weighed today: ____________

Daily "to-do's": *shopping/errands/home tasks/etc*

Memorable Headlines or Event of the Day: *(current event from the news or in my own life)*

**Baby Countdown: 21 weeks to go**

Due Date: ____________

Date: ______________________

## Daily Encouragement

*God is bigger than your problems. Whatever worries press upon you today, put them in God's hands and leave them there.*

BILLY GRAHAM

Appointments today: *Doctors/Dentist/Hair/Nails/etc.*

______________________

______________________

What I'm feeling in my heart and spirit:

______________________

______________________

What I'm feeling physically:

______________________

______________________

What I ate today:

______________________

______________________

What I weighed today: ______________________

Daily "to-do's": *shopping/errands/home tasks/etc*

______________________

______________________

Memorable Headlines or Event of the Day: *(current event from the news or in my own life)*

______________________

______________________

**Baby Countdown: 21 weeks to go**

Due Date: ______________________

WEEK NINETEEN Date: ____________

## DAILY ENCOURAGEMENT

*But an hour is coming, and is now here, when the true worshipers will worship the Father in spirit and truth. Yes, the Father wants such people to worship Him. God is Spirit, and those who worship Him must worship in spirit and truth.*

JOHN 4:23-24 HCSB

Appointments today: *Doctors/Dentist/Hair/Nails/etc.*

What I'm feeling in my heart and spirit:

What I'm feeling physically:

What I ate today:

What I weighed today: ____________

Daily "to-do's": *shopping/errands/home tasks/etc*

Memorable Headlines or Event of the Day: *(current event from the news or in my own life)*

**Baby Countdown: 21 weeks to go**

Due Date: ____________

Week Nineteen

## *Personal Journal*

You know my heart Lord...

## *A Mother's Prayer:*

Precious baby, I pray for you, I care for you, I love you...

Week Twenty Date: ______________________

## Daily Encouragement

*He is ever faithful and gives us the song in the night to soothe our spirits and fresh joy each morning to lift our souls. What a marvelous Lord!*

BILL BRIGHT

Appointments today: *Doctors/Dentist/Hair/Nails/etc.*

______________________

______________________

What I'm feeling in my heart and spirit:

______________________

______________________

What I'm feeling physically:

______________________

______________________

What I ate today:

______________________

______________________

What I weighed today: ______________________

Daily "to-do's": *shopping/errands/home tasks/etc*

______________________

______________________

Memorable Headlines or Event of the Day: *(current event from the news or in my own life)*

______________________

______________________

**Baby Countdown: 20 weeks to go**

Due Date: ______________________

Week Twenty                    *Date:* ______________________

## Daily Encouragement

*Now I am coming to You, and I speak these things in the world so that they may have My joy completed in them.*

JOHN 17:13 HCSB

Appointments today: *Doctors/Dentist/Hair/Nails/etc.*

______________________________________________

______________________________________________

What I'm feeling in my heart and spirit:

______________________________________________

______________________________________________

What I'm feeling physically:

______________________________________________

______________________________________________

What I ate today:

______________________________________________

______________________________________________

What I weighed today: ______________________________

Daily "to-do's": *shopping/errands/home tasks/etc*

______________________________________________

______________________________________________

Memorable Headlines or Event of the Day: *(current event from the news or in my own life)*

______________________________________________

______________________________________________

**Baby Countdown: 20 weeks to go**

Due Date: ______________________

Week Twenty Date: ____________________

## Daily Encouragement

*The Bible is a remarkable commentary on perspective. Through its divine message, we are brought face to face with issues and tests in daily living and how, by the power of the Holy Spirit, we are enabled to respond positively to them.*

LUCI SWINDOLL

Appointments today: *Doctors/Dentist/Hair/Nails/etc.*

______________________________

______________________________

What I'm feeling in my heart and spirit:

______________________________

______________________________

What I'm feeling physically:

______________________________

______________________________

What I ate today:

______________________________

______________________________

What I weighed today: ____________________

Daily "to-do's": *shopping/errands/home tasks/etc*

______________________________

______________________________

Memorable Headlines or Event of the Day: *(current event from the news or in my own life)*

______________________________

______________________________

**Baby Countdown: 20 weeks to go**

Due Date: ____________________

WEEK TWENTY                    *Date:* ______________________

## DAILY ENCOURAGEMENT

*God has chosen you and made you his holy people. He loves you. So always do these things: Show mercy to others, be kind, humble, gentle, and patient.*

COLOSSIANS 3:12 NCV

Appointments today: *Doctors/Dentist/Hair/Nails/etc.*

______________________________________________

______________________________________________

What I'm feeling in my heart and spirit:

______________________________________________

______________________________________________

What I'm feeling physically:

______________________________________________

______________________________________________

What I ate today:

______________________________________________

______________________________________________

What I weighed today: ______________________________

Daily "to-do's": *shopping/errands/home tasks/etc*

______________________________________________

______________________________________________

Memorable Headlines or Event of the Day: *(current event from the news or in my own life)*

______________________________________________

______________________________________________

**Baby Countdown: 20 weeks to go**

Due Date: ____________________

Week Twenty Date: ______________________

## Daily Encouragement

*Hope looks for the good in people, opens doors for people, discovers what can be done to help, lights a candle, does not yield to cynicism. Hope sets people free.*

BARBARA JOHNSON

Appointments today: *Doctors/Dentist/Hair/Nails/etc.*

______________________

______________________

What I'm feeling in my heart and spirit:

______________________

______________________

What I'm feeling physically:

______________________

______________________

What I ate today:

______________________

______________________

What I weighed today: ______________________

Daily "to-do's": *shopping/errands/home tasks/etc*

______________________

______________________

Memorable Headlines or Event of the Day: *(current event from the news or in my own life)*

______________________

______________________

**Baby Countdown: 20 weeks to go**

Due Date: ______________________

## Personal Journal

You know my heart Lord…

## A Mother's Prayer:

Precious baby, I pray for you, I care for you, I love you…

## Week Twenty-One

*Date:* ______________________

### Daily Encouragement

*Therefore as you have received Christ Jesus the Lord, walk in Him.*

COLOSSIANS 2:6 HCSB

Appointments today: *Doctors/Dentist/Hair/Nails/etc.*

______________________

______________________

What I'm feeling in my heart and spirit:

______________________

______________________

What I'm feeling physically:

______________________

______________________

What I ate today:

______________________

______________________

What I weighed today: ______________________

Daily "to-do's": *shopping/errands/home tasks/etc*

______________________

______________________

Memorable Headlines or Event of the Day: *(current event from the news or in my own life)*

______________________

______________________

**Baby Countdown: 19 weeks to go**

Due Date: ______________________

WEEK TWENTY-ONE Date: ____________________

## DAILY ENCOURAGEMENT

*The Christian faith is meant to be lived moment by moment. It isn't some broad, general outline—it's a long walk with a real Person.*

JONI EARECKSON TADA

Appointments today: *Doctors/Dentist/Hair/Nails/etc.*

______________________________________________

______________________________________________

What I'm feeling in my heart and spirit:

______________________________________________

______________________________________________

What I'm feeling physically:

______________________________________________

______________________________________________

What I ate today:

______________________________________________

______________________________________________

What I weighed today: ______________________________

Daily "to-do's": *shopping/errands/home tasks/etc*

______________________________________________

______________________________________________

Memorable Headlines or Event of the Day: *(current event from the news or in my own life)*

______________________________________________

______________________________________________

**Baby Countdown: 19 weeks to go**

Due Date: ____________________

## Week Twenty-One Date: ______________________

### Daily Encouragement

*The Lord is my rock and my fortress and my deliverer; the God of my strength, in whom I will trust.*

2 SAMUEL 22:2-3 NKJV

Appointments today: *Doctors/Dentist/Hair/Nails/etc.*

______________________

______________________

What I'm feeling in my heart and spirit:

______________________

______________________

What I'm feeling physically:

______________________

______________________

What I ate today:

______________________

______________________

What I weighed today: ______________________

Daily "to-do's": *shopping/errands/home tasks/etc*

______________________

______________________

Memorable Headlines or Event of the Day: *(current event from the news or in my own life)*

______________________

______________________

**Baby Countdown: 19 weeks to go**

Due Date: ______________________

WEEK TWENTY-ONE *Date:* ______________________

## DAILY ENCOURAGEMENT

*Look around you and you'll be distressed; look within yourself and you'll be depressed; look at Jesus, and you'll be at rest!*

CORRIE TEN BOOM

Appointments today: *Doctors/Dentist/Hair/Nails/etc.*

What I'm feeling in my heart and spirit:

What I'm feeling physically:

What I ate today:

What I weighed today: ______________________

Daily "to-do's": *shopping/errands/home tasks/etc*

Memorable Headlines or Event of the Day: *(current event from the news or in my own life)*

**Baby Countdown: 19 weeks to go**

Due Date: ______________________

WEEK TWENTY-ONE   *Date:* ____________________

## DAILY ENCOURAGEMENT

*I have learned to be content whatever the circumstances.*

PHILIPPIANS 4:11 NIV

Appointments today: *Doctors/Dentist/Hair/Nails/etc.*

---

---

What I'm feeling in my heart and spirit:

---

---

What I'm feeling physically:

---

---

What I ate today:

---

---

What I weighed today: ____________________

Daily "to-do's": *shopping/errands/home tasks/etc*

---

---

Memorable Headlines or Event of the Day: *(current event from the news or in my own life)*

---

---

**Baby Countdown: 19 weeks to go**

Due Date: ____________________

Week Twenty-One

## Personal Journal

You know my heart Lord…

## A Mother's Prayer:

Precious baby, I pray for you, I care for you, I love you…

Week Twenty-Two Date: ______________________

## Daily Encouragement

*Faith is the willingness to receive whatever he wants to give, or the willingness not to have what he does not want to give.*

Elisabeth Elliot

Appointments today: *Doctors/Dentist/Hair/Nails/etc.*

______________________

______________________

What I'm feeling in my heart and spirit:

______________________

______________________

What I'm feeling physically:

______________________

______________________

What I ate today:

______________________

______________________

What I weighed today: ______________________

Daily "to-do's": *shopping/errands/home tasks/etc*

______________________

______________________

Memorable Headlines or Event of the Day: *(current event from the news or in my own life)*

______________________

______________________

**Baby Countdown: 18 weeks to go**

Due Date: ______________________

## Week Twenty-Two

*Date:* ______________________

### Daily Encouragement

*The heavens declare the glory of God; and the firmament shows His handiwork.*

PSALM 19:1 NKJV

Appointments today: *Doctors/Dentist/Hair/Nails/etc.*

______________________

______________________

What I'm feeling in my heart and spirit:

______________________

______________________

What I'm feeling physically:

______________________

______________________

What I ate today:

______________________

______________________

What I weighed today: ______________________

Daily "to-do's": *shopping/errands/home tasks/etc*

______________________

______________________

Memorable Headlines or Event of the Day: *(current event from the news or in my own life)*

______________________

______________________

**Baby Countdown: 18 weeks to go**

Due Date: ______________________

WEEK TWENTY-TWO Date: ____________________

## DAILY ENCOURAGEMENT

*Heaven and earth and all that is in the universe cry out to me from all directions that I, O God, must love You.*

ST. AUGUSTINE

Appointments today: *Doctors/Dentist/Hair/Nails/etc.*

What I'm feeling in my heart and spirit:

What I'm feeling physically:

What I ate today:

What I weighed today: ____________________

Daily "to-do's": *shopping/errands/home tasks/etc*

Memorable Headlines or Event of the Day: *(current event from the news or in my own life)*

**Baby Countdown: 18 weeks to go**

Due Date: ____________________

## Week Twenty-Two

*Date:* ____________________

### Daily Encouragement

*In thee, O Lord, do I put my trust.*

PSALM 31:1 KJV

Appointments today: *Doctors/Dentist/Hair/Nails/etc.*

______________________________

______________________________

What I'm feeling in my heart and spirit:

______________________________

______________________________

What I'm feeling physically:

______________________________

______________________________

What I ate today:

______________________________

______________________________

What I weighed today: ____________________

Daily "to-do's": *shopping/errands/home tasks/etc*

______________________________

______________________________

Memorable Headlines or Event of the Day: *(current event from the news or in my own life)*

______________________________

______________________________

**Baby Countdown: 18 weeks to go**

Due Date: ____________________

WEEK TWENTY-TWO Date: ____________________

## DAILY ENCOURAGEMENT

*Worship and worry cannot live in the same heart; they are mutually exclusive.*

RUTH BELL GRAHAM

Appointments today: *Doctors/Dentist/Hair/Nails/etc.*

____________________

____________________

What I'm feeling in my heart and spirit:

____________________

____________________

What I'm feeling physically:

____________________

____________________

What I ate today:

____________________

____________________

What I weighed today: ____________________

Daily "to-do's": *shopping/errands/home tasks/etc*

____________________

____________________

Memorable Headlines or Event of the Day: *(current event from the news or in my own life)*

____________________

____________________

**Baby Countdown: 18 weeks to go**

Due Date: ____________________

WEEK TWENTY-TWO

## Personal Journal

YOU KNOW MY HEART LORD...

## A Mother's Prayer:

PRECIOUS BABY, I PRAY FOR YOU, I CARE FOR YOU, I LOVE YOU...

Week Twenty-Three Date: ______________________

## Daily Encouragement

*In everything give thanks; for this is the will of God in Christ Jesus for you.*

1 THESSALONIANS 5:18 NKJV

Appointments today: *Doctors/Dentist/Hair/Nails/etc.*

______________________

______________________

What I'm feeling in my heart and spirit:

______________________

______________________

What I'm feeling physically:

______________________

______________________

What I ate today:

______________________

______________________

What I weighed today: ______________________

Daily "to-do's": *shopping/errands/home tasks/etc*

______________________

______________________

Memorable Headlines or Event of the Day: *(current event from the news or in my own life)*

______________________

______________________

**Baby Countdown: 17 weeks to go**

Due Date: ______________________

Week Twenty-Three

*Date:* ____________________

## Daily Encouragement

*No duty is more urgent than that of returning thanks.*

ST. AMBROSE

Appointments today: *Doctors/Dentist/Hair/Nails/etc.*

What I'm feeling in my heart and spirit:

What I'm feeling physically:

What I ate today:

What I weighed today: ____________________

Daily "to-do's": *shopping/errands/home tasks/etc*

Memorable Headlines or Event of the Day: *(current event from the news or in my own life)*

**Baby Countdown: 17 weeks to go**

Due Date: ____________________

Week Twenty-Three Date: ______________________

Daily Encouragement

*Wait on the Lord, and He will rescue you.*

PROVERBS 20:22 HCSB

Appointments today: *Doctors/Dentist/Hair/Nails/etc.*

______________________

______________________

What I'm feeling in my heart and spirit:

______________________

______________________

What I'm feeling physically:

______________________

______________________

What I ate today:

______________________

______________________

What I weighed today: ______________________

Daily "to-do's": *shopping/errands/home tasks/etc*

______________________

______________________

Memorable Headlines or Event of the Day: *(current event from the news or in my own life)*

______________________

______________________

**Baby Countdown: 17 weeks to go**

Due Date: ______________________

## Week Twenty-Three

Date: ______________________

### Daily Encouragement

*God has a designated time when his promise will be fulfilled and the prayer will be answered.*

JIM CYMBALA

Appointments today: *Doctors/Dentist/Hair/Nails/etc.*

______________________

______________________

What I'm feeling in my heart and spirit:

______________________

______________________

What I'm feeling physically:

______________________

______________________

What I ate today:

______________________

______________________

What I weighed today: ______________________

Daily "to-do's": *shopping/errands/home tasks/etc*

______________________

______________________

Memorable Headlines or Event of the Day: *(current event from the news or in my own life)*

______________________

______________________

**Baby Countdown: 17 weeks to go**

Due Date: ______________________

WEEK TWENTY-THREE Date: ______________

## DAILY ENCOURAGEMENT

*Watch therefore, and pray always that you may be counted worthy . . . .*

LUKE 21:36 NKJV

Appointments today: *Doctors/Dentist/Hair/Nails/etc.*

What I'm feeling in my heart and spirit:

What I'm feeling physically:

What I ate today:

What I weighed today: ______________

Daily "to-do's": *shopping/errands/home tasks/etc*

Memorable Headlines or Event of the Day: *(current event from the news or in my own life)*

**Baby Countdown: 17 weeks to go**

Due Date: ______________

Week Twenty-Three

## *Personal Journal*

You know my heart Lord…

## *A Mother's Prayer:*

Precious baby, I pray for you, I care for you, I love you…

Week Twenty-Four Date: ______________________

## Daily Encouragement

*When we pray, we have linked ourselves with Divine purposes, and we therefore have Divine power at our disposal for human living.*

E. STANLEY JONES

Appointments today: *Doctors/Dentist/Hair/Nails/etc.*

What I'm feeling in my heart and spirit:

What I'm feeling physically:

What I ate today:

What I weighed today: ______________________

Daily "to-do's": *shopping/errands/home tasks/etc*

Memorable Headlines or Event of the Day: *(current event from the news or in my own life)*

**Baby Countdown: 16 weeks to go**

Due Date: ______________________

## Week Twenty-Four

Date: ____________________

### Daily Encouragement

*May the God of hope fill you with all joy and peace as you trust in him, so that you may overflow with hope by the power of the Holy Spirit.*

ROMANS 15:13 NIV

Appointments today: *Doctors/Dentist/Hair/Nails/etc.*

What I'm feeling in my heart and spirit:

What I'm feeling physically:

What I ate today:

What I weighed today: ____________________

Daily "to-do's": *shopping/errands/home tasks/etc*

Memorable Headlines or Event of the Day: *(current event from the news or in my own life)*

**Baby Countdown: 16 weeks to go**

Due Date: ____________________

## Week Twenty-Four

Date: ____________________

### Daily Encouragement

*To know God as He really is—in His essential nature and character—is to arrive at a citadel of peace that circumstances may storm, but can never capture.*

CATHERINE MARSHALL

Appointments today: *Doctors/Dentist/Hair/Nails/etc.*

What I'm feeling in my heart and spirit:

What I'm feeling physically:

What I ate today:

What I weighed today: ____________________

Daily "to-do's": *shopping/errands/home tasks/etc*

Memorable Headlines or Event of the Day: *(current event from the news or in my own life)*

**Baby Countdown: 16 weeks to go**

Due Date: ____________________

## Week Twenty-Four

*Date:* ______________________

### Daily Encouragement

*At the name of Jesus every knee should bow, of those in heaven, and of those on earth, and of those under the earth, and that every tongue should confess that Jesus Christ is Lord, to the glory of God the Father.*

PHILIPPIANS 2:10-11 NKJV

Appointments today: *Doctors/Dentist/Hair/Nails/etc.*

______________________

______________________

What I'm feeling in my heart and spirit:

______________________

______________________

What I'm feeling physically:

______________________

______________________

What I ate today:

______________________

______________________

What I weighed today: ______________________

Daily "to-do's": *shopping/errands/home tasks/etc*

______________________

______________________

Memorable Headlines or Event of the Day: *(current event from the news or in my own life)*

______________________

______________________

**Baby Countdown: 16 weeks to go**

Due Date: ______________________

## Week Twenty-Four

*Date:* ______________________

### Daily Encouragement

*The time for universal praise is sure to come some day. Let us begin to do our part now.*

HANNAH WHITALL SMITH

Appointments today: *Doctors/Dentist/Hair/Nails/etc.*

______________________

______________________

What I'm feeling in my heart and spirit:

______________________

______________________

What I'm feeling physically:

______________________

______________________

What I ate today:

______________________

______________________

What I weighed today: ______________________

Daily "to-do's": *shopping/errands/home tasks/etc*

______________________

______________________

Memorable Headlines or Event of the Day: *(current event from the news or in my own life)*

______________________

______________________

**Baby Countdown: 16 weeks to go**

Due Date: ______________________

WEEK TWENTY-FOUR

## *Personal Journal*

YOU KNOW MY HEART LORD...

## *A Mother's Prayer:*

PRECIOUS BABY, I PRAY FOR YOU, I CARE FOR YOU, I LOVE YOU...

Week Twenty-Five Date: ____________________

## Daily Encouragement

*Teach us to number our days carefully so that we may develop wisdom in our hearts.*

PSALM 90:12 HCSB

Appointments today: *Doctors/Dentist/Hair/Nails/etc.*

What I'm feeling in my heart and spirit:

What I'm feeling physically:

What I ate today:

What I weighed today: ____________________

Daily "to-do's": *shopping/errands/home tasks/etc*

Memorable Headlines or Event of the Day: *(current event from the news or in my own life)*

**Baby Countdown: 15 weeks to go**

Due Date: ____________________

## Week Twenty-Five

*Date:* ______________________

### Daily Encouragement

*Live today fully, expressing gratitude for all you have been, all you are right now, and all you are becoming.*

MELODIE BEATTIE

Appointments today: *Doctors/Dentist/Hair/Nails/etc.*

______________________

______________________

What I'm feeling in my heart and spirit:

______________________

______________________

What I'm feeling physically:

______________________

______________________

What I ate today:

______________________

______________________

What I weighed today: ______________________

Daily "to-do's": *shopping/errands/home tasks/etc*

______________________

______________________

Memorable Headlines or Event of the Day: *(current event from the news or in my own life)*

______________________

______________________

**Baby Countdown: 15 weeks to go**

Due Date: ______________________

Week Twenty-Five    *Date:* ____________________

## Daily Encouragement

*When I am filled with cares, Your comfort brings me joy.*

PSALM 94:19 HCSB

Appointments today: *Doctors/Dentist/Hair/Nails/etc.*

What I'm feeling in my heart and spirit:

What I'm feeling physically:

What I ate today:

What I weighed today: ____________________

Daily "to-do's": *shopping/errands/home tasks/etc*

Memorable Headlines or Event of the Day: *(current event from the news or in my own life)*

**Baby Countdown: 15 weeks to go**

Due Date: ____________________

WEEK TWENTY-FIVE Date: ____________

## DAILY ENCOURAGEMENT

*When God allows extraordinary trials for His people, He prepares extraordinary comforts for them.*

CORRIE TEN BOOM

Appointments today: *Doctors/Dentist/Hair/Nails/etc.*

What I'm feeling in my heart and spirit:

What I'm feeling physically:

What I ate today:

What I weighed today: ____________

Daily "to-do's": *shopping/errands/home tasks/etc*

Memorable Headlines or Event of the Day: *(current event from the news or in my own life)*

**Baby Countdown: 15 weeks to go**

Due Date: ____________

Week Twenty-Five Date: ______________________

## Daily Encouragement

*He has made everything beautiful in its time.*

ECCLESIASTES 3:11 NKJV

Appointments today: *Doctors/Dentist/Hair/Nails/etc.*

______________________________________________

______________________________________________

What I'm feeling in my heart and spirit:

______________________________________________

______________________________________________

What I'm feeling physically:

______________________________________________

______________________________________________

What I ate today:

______________________________________________

______________________________________________

What I weighed today: ______________________________

Daily "to-do's": *shopping/errands/home tasks/etc*

______________________________________________

______________________________________________

Memorable Headlines or Event of the Day: *(current event from the news or in my own life)*

______________________________________________

______________________________________________

**Baby Countdown: 15 weeks to go**

Due Date: ______________________

Week Twenty-Five

## Personal Journal

You know my heart Lord…

## A Mother's Prayer:

Precious baby, I pray for you, I care for you, I love you…

Week Twenty-Six Date: ______________________

## Daily Encouragement

*Your times are in His hands. He's in charge of the timetable, so wait patiently.*

KAY ARTHUR

Appointments today: *Doctors/Dentist/Hair/Nails/etc.*

What I'm feeling in my heart and spirit:

What I'm feeling physically:

What I ate today:

What I weighed today: ______________________

Daily "to-do's": *shopping/errands/home tasks/etc*

Memorable Headlines or Event of the Day: *(current event from the news or in my own life)*

**Baby Countdown: 14 weeks to go**

Due Date: ______________________

Week Twenty-Six Date: ____________________

## Daily Encouragement

*The Lord is my light and my salvation; whom shall I fear? The Lord is the strength of my life; of whom shall I be afraid?*

PSALM 27:1 NKJV

Appointments today: *Doctors/Dentist/Hair/Nails/etc.*

What I'm feeling in my heart and spirit:

What I'm feeling physically:

What I ate today:

What I weighed today: ____________________

Daily "to-do's": *shopping/errands/home tasks/etc*

Memorable Headlines or Event of the Day: *(current event from the news or in my own life)*

**Baby Countdown: 14 weeks to go**

Due Date: ____________________

WEEK TWENTY-SIX *Date:* ______________

## DAILY ENCOURAGEMENT

*If a person fears God, he or she has no reason to fear anything else. On the other hand, if a person does not fear God, then fear becomes a way of life.*

BETH MOORE

Appointments today: *Doctors/Dentist/Hair/Nails/etc.*

What I'm feeling in my heart and spirit:

What I'm feeling physically:

What I ate today:

What I weighed today: ______________

Daily "to-do's": *shopping/errands/home tasks/etc*

Memorable Headlines or Event of the Day: *(current event from the news or in my own life)*

**Baby Countdown: 14 weeks to go**

Due Date: ______________

WEEK TWENTY-SIX Date: ____________________

## DAILY ENCOURAGEMENT

*The LORD is my strength and my song; he has become my victory.
He is my God, and I will praise him.*

EXODUS 15:2 NLT

Appointments today: *Doctors/Dentist/Hair/Nails/etc.*

______________________________________________

______________________________________________

What I'm feeling in my heart and spirit:

______________________________________________

______________________________________________

What I'm feeling physically:

______________________________________________

______________________________________________

What I ate today:

______________________________________________

______________________________________________

What I weighed today: ____________________

Daily "to-do's": *shopping/errands/home tasks/etc*

______________________________________________

______________________________________________

Memorable Headlines or Event of the Day: *(current event from the news or in my own life)*

______________________________________________

______________________________________________

**Baby Countdown: 14 weeks to go**

Due Date: ____________________

Week Twenty-Six Date: ______________________

## Daily Encouragement

*Faith is taking God at His Word. No matter how you feel, no matter how you read the circumstances, no matter what anyone else tells you about the truthfulness of what God says. God is truthful.*

KAY ARTHUR

Appointments today: *Doctors/Dentist/Hair/Nails/etc.*

______________________

______________________

What I'm feeling in my heart and spirit:

______________________

______________________

What I'm feeling physically:

______________________

______________________

What I ate today:

______________________

______________________

What I weighed today: ______________________

Daily "to-do's": *shopping/errands/home tasks/etc*

______________________

______________________

Memorable Headlines or Event of the Day: *(current event from the news or in my own life)*

______________________

______________________

**Baby Countdown: 14 weeks to go**

Due Date: ______________________

WEEK TWENTY-SIX

## Personal Journal

YOU KNOW MY HEART LORD...

## A Mother's Prayer:

PRECIOUS BABY, I PRAY FOR YOU, I CARE FOR YOU, I LOVE YOU...

WEEK TWENTY-SEVEN Date: ____________________

## DAILY ENCOURAGEMENT

*The Lord is my rock, my fortress, and my deliverer.*

PSALM 18:2 HCSB

Appointments today: *Doctors/Dentist/Hair/Nails/etc.*

___

___

What I'm feeling in my heart and spirit:

___

___

What I'm feeling physically:

___

___

What I ate today:

___

___

What I weighed today: ____________________

Daily "to-do's": *shopping/errands/home tasks/etc*

___

___

Memorable Headlines or Event of the Day: *(current event from the news or in my own life)*

___

___

**Baby Countdown: 13 weeks to go**

Due Date: ____________________

Week Twenty-Seven                    *Date:* ______________________

## Daily Encouragement

*The Rock of Ages is the great sheltering encirclement.*

OSWALD CHAMBERS

Appointments today: *Doctors/Dentist/Hair/Nails/etc.*

______________________________________________

______________________________________________

What I'm feeling in my heart and spirit:

______________________________________________

______________________________________________

What I'm feeling physically:

______________________________________________

______________________________________________

What I ate today:

______________________________________________

______________________________________________

What I weighed today: ______________________________

Daily "to-do's": *shopping/errands/home tasks/etc*

______________________________________________

______________________________________________

Memorable Headlines or Event of the Day: *(current event from the news or in my own life)*

______________________________________________

______________________________________________

**Baby Countdown: 13 weeks to go**

Due Date: ______________________

Week Twenty-Seven Date: ______________________

## Daily Encouragement

*Love is patient, love is kind and is not jealous; love does not brag and is not arrogant, does not act unbecomingly; it does not seek its own, is not provoked, does not take into account a wrong suffered, does not rejoice in unrighteousness, but rejoices with the truth; bears all things, believes all things, hopes all things, endures all things.*

1 CORINTHIANS 13:4-7 NASB

Appointments today: *Doctors/Dentist/Hair/Nails/etc.*

______________________________________________

______________________________________________

What I'm feeling in my heart and spirit:

______________________________________________

______________________________________________

What I'm feeling physically:

______________________________________________

______________________________________________

What I ate today:

______________________________________________

______________________________________________

What I weighed today: ______________________________

Daily "to-do's": *shopping/errands/home tasks/etc*

______________________________________________

______________________________________________

Memorable Headlines or Event of the Day: *(current event from the news or in my own life)*

______________________________________________

______________________________________________

**Baby Countdown: 13 weeks to go**

Due Date: ______________________

## Week Twenty-Seven

*Date:* ______________________

### Daily Encouragement

*The first essential for a happy home is love.*

BILLY GRAHAM

Appointments today: *Doctors/Dentist/Hair/Nails/etc.*

______________________

______________________

What I'm feeling in my heart and spirit:

______________________

______________________

What I'm feeling physically:

______________________

______________________

What I ate today:

______________________

______________________

What I weighed today: ______________________

Daily "to-do's": *shopping/errands/home tasks/etc*

______________________

______________________

Memorable Headlines or Event of the Day: *(current event from the news or in my own life)*

______________________

______________________

**Baby Countdown: 13 weeks to go**

Due Date: ______________________

## Week Twenty-Seven Date: ____________________

### Daily Encouragement

*Shout triumphantly to the Lord, all the earth. Serve the Lord with gladness; come before Him with joyful songs.*

PSALM 100:1-2 HCSB

Appointments today: *Doctors/Dentist/Hair/Nails/etc.*

What I'm feeling in my heart and spirit:

What I'm feeling physically:

What I ate today:

What I weighed today: ____________________

Daily "to-do's": *shopping/errands/home tasks/etc*

Memorable Headlines or Event of the Day: *(current event from the news or in my own life)*

**Baby Countdown: 13 weeks to go**

Due Date: ____________________

Week Twenty-Seven

## Personal Journal

You know my heart Lord…

## A Mother's Prayer:

Precious baby, I pray for you, I care for you, I love you…

Week Twenty-Eight Date: ______________________

## Daily Encouragement

*When we invite Jesus into our lives, we experience life in the fullest, most vital sense.*

CATHERINE MARSHALL

Appointments today: *Doctors/Dentist/Hair/Nails/etc.*

______________________

______________________

What I'm feeling in my heart and spirit:

______________________

______________________

What I'm feeling physically:

______________________

______________________

What I ate today:

______________________

______________________

What I weighed today: ______________________

Daily "to-do's": *shopping/errands/home tasks/etc*

______________________

______________________

Memorable Headlines or Event of the Day: *(current event from the news or in my own life)*

______________________

______________________

**Baby Countdown: 12 weeks to go**

Due Date: ______________________

## Week Twenty-Eight

*Date:* ______________________

### Daily Encouragement

*But the wisdom that is from above is first pure, then peaceable, gentle, willing to yield, full of mercy and good fruits, without partiality and without hypocrisy.*

JAMES 3:17 NKJV

Appointments today: *Doctors/Dentist/Hair/Nails/etc.*

______________________

______________________

What I'm feeling in my heart and spirit:

______________________

______________________

What I'm feeling physically:

______________________

______________________

What I ate today:

______________________

______________________

What I weighed today: ______________________

Daily "to-do's": *shopping/errands/home tasks/etc*

______________________

______________________

Memorable Headlines or Event of the Day: *(current event from the news or in my own life)*

______________________

______________________

**Baby Countdown: 12 weeks to go**

Due Date: ______________________

WEEK TWENTY-EIGHT Date: ______________________

## DAILY ENCOURAGEMENT

*Be so preoccupied with good will that you haven't room for ill will.*

E. STANLEY JONES

Appointments today: *Doctors/Dentist/Hair/Nails/etc.*

______________________

______________________

What I'm feeling in my heart and spirit:

______________________

______________________

What I'm feeling physically:

______________________

______________________

What I ate today:

______________________

______________________

What I weighed today: ______________________

Daily "to-do's": *shopping/errands/home tasks/etc*

______________________

______________________

Memorable Headlines or Event of the Day: *(current event from the news or in my own life)*

______________________

______________________

**Baby Countdown: 12 weeks to go**

Due Date: ______________________

## Week Twenty-Eight

Date: ____________

### Daily Encouragement

*Do everything without complaining or arguing. Then you will be innocent and without any wrong.*

PHILIPPIANS 2:14-15 NCV

Appointments today: *Doctors/Dentist/Hair/Nails/etc.*

What I'm feeling in my heart and spirit:

What I'm feeling physically:

What I ate today:

What I weighed today: ____________

Daily "to-do's": *shopping/errands/home tasks/etc*

Memorable Headlines or Event of the Day: *(current event from the news or in my own life)*

**Baby Countdown: 12 weeks to go**

Due Date: ____________

## Week Twenty-Eight

Date: ______________________

### Daily Encouragement

*Thanksgiving or complaining—these words express two contrastive attitudes of the souls of God's children in regard to His dealings with them. The soul that gives thanks can find comfort in everything; the soul that complains can find comfort in nothing.*

HANNAH WHITALL SMITH

Appointments today: *Doctors/Dentist/Hair/Nails/etc.*

______________________

______________________

What I'm feeling in my heart and spirit:

______________________

______________________

What I'm feeling physically:

______________________

______________________

What I ate today:

______________________

______________________

What I weighed today: ______________________

Daily "to-do's": *shopping/errands/home tasks/etc*

______________________

______________________

Memorable Headlines or Event of the Day: *(current event from the news or in my own life)*

______________________

______________________

**Baby Countdown: 12 weeks to go**

Due Date: ______________________

Week Twenty-Eight

## *Personal Journal*

You know my heart Lord...

## *A Mother's Prayer:*

Precious baby, I pray for you, I care for you, I love you...

## Week Twenty-Nine

*Date:* ______

### Daily Encouragement

*So encourage each other and give each other strength, just as you are doing now.*

1 THESSALONIANS 5:11 NCV

Appointments today: *Doctors/Dentist/Hair/Nails/etc.*

______

______

What I'm feeling in my heart and spirit:

______

______

What I'm feeling physically:

______

______

What I ate today:

______

______

What I weighed today: ______

Daily "to-do's": *shopping/errands/home tasks/etc*

______

______

Memorable Headlines or Event of the Day: *(current event from the news or in my own life)*

______

______

**Baby Countdown: 11 weeks to go**

Due Date: ______

## Week Twenty-Nine

Date: ______________________

### Daily Encouragement

*Those who keep speaking about the sun while walking under a cloudy sky are messengers of hope, the true saints of our day.*

Henri Nouwen

Appointments today: *Doctors/Dentist/Hair/Nails/etc.*

______________________

______________________

What I'm feeling in my heart and spirit:

______________________

______________________

What I'm feeling physically:

______________________

______________________

What I ate today:

______________________

______________________

What I weighed today: ______________________

Daily "to-do's": *shopping/errands/home tasks/etc*

______________________

______________________

Memorable Headlines or Event of the Day: *(current event from the news or in my own life)*

______________________

______________________

**Baby Countdown: 11 weeks to go**

Due Date: ______________________

WEEK TWENTY-NINE Date: ____________

## DAILY ENCOURAGEMENT

*Have faith in the Lord your God, and you will stand strong.*
*Have faith in his prophets, and you will succeed.*

2 CHRONICLES 20:20 NCV

Appointments today: *Doctors/Dentist/Hair/Nails/etc.*

What I'm feeling in my heart and spirit:

What I'm feeling physically:

What I ate today:

What I weighed today: ____________

Daily "to-do's": *shopping/errands/home tasks/etc*

Memorable Headlines or Event of the Day: *(current event from the news or in my own life)*

**Baby Countdown: 11 weeks to go**

Due Date: ____________

Week Twenty-Nine Date: ______________________

## Daily Encouragement

*Shout the shout of faith. Nothing can withstand the triumphant faith that links itself to omnipotence. For "this is the victory that overcometh the world." The secret of all successful living lies in this shout of faith.*

Hannah Whitall Smith

Appointments today: *Doctors/Dentist/Hair/Nails/etc.*

______________________

______________________

What I'm feeling in my heart and spirit:

______________________

______________________

What I'm feeling physically:

______________________

______________________

What I ate today:

______________________

______________________

What I weighed today: ______________________

Daily "to-do's": *shopping/errands/home tasks/etc*

______________________

______________________

Memorable Headlines or Event of the Day: *(current event from the news or in my own life)*

______________________

______________________

**Baby Countdown: 11 weeks to go**

Due Date: ______________________

Week Twenty-Nine Date: ____________________

## Daily Encouragement

*Until now you have not asked for anything in my name.*
*Ask and you will receive, so that your joy will be the fullest possible joy.*

JOHN 16:24 NCV

Appointments today: *Doctors/Dentist/Hair/Nails/etc.*

What I'm feeling in my heart and spirit:

What I'm feeling physically:

What I ate today:

What I weighed today: ____________________

Daily "to-do's": *shopping/errands/home tasks/etc*

Memorable Headlines or Event of the Day: *(current event from the news or in my own life)*

**Baby Countdown: 11 weeks to go**

Due Date: ____________________

Week Twenty-Nine

## *Personal Journal*

You know my heart Lord...

## *A Mother's Prayer:*

Precious baby, I pray for you, I care for you, I love you...

WEEK THIRTY Date: ______________________

## DAILY ENCOURAGEMENT

*Don't be afraid to ask your heavenly Father for anything you need. Indeed, nothing is too small for God's attention or too great for his power.*

DENNIS SWANBERG

Appointments today: *Doctors/Dentist/Hair/Nails/etc.*

______________________

______________________

What I'm feeling in my heart and spirit:

______________________

______________________

What I'm feeling physically:

______________________

______________________

What I ate today:

______________________

______________________

What I weighed today: ______________________

Daily "to-do's": *shopping/errands/home tasks/etc*

______________________

______________________

Memorable Headlines or Event of the Day: *(current event from the news or in my own life)*

______________________

______________________

**Baby Countdown: 10 weeks to go**

Due Date: ______________________

WEEK THIRTY  *Date:* ______________________

## DAILY ENCOURAGEMENT

*I assure you: If anyone says to this mountain, "Be lifted up and thrown into the sea," and does not doubt in his heart, but believes that what he says will happen, it will be done for him.*

MARK 11:23 HCSB

Appointments today: *Doctors/Dentist/Hair/Nails/etc.*

What I'm feeling in my heart and spirit:

What I'm feeling physically:

What I ate today:

What I weighed today: ______________________

Daily "to-do's": *shopping/errands/home tasks/etc*

Memorable Headlines or Event of the Day: *(current event from the news or in my own life)*

**Baby Countdown: 10 weeks to go**

Due Date: ______________________

WEEK THIRTY    *Date:* ____________________

## DAILY ENCOURAGEMENT

*Faith is deliberate confidence in the character of God whose ways you cannot understand at the time.*

OSWALD CHAMBERS

Appointments today: *Doctors/Dentist/Hair/Nails/etc.*

____________________

____________________

What I'm feeling in my heart and spirit:

____________________

____________________

What I'm feeling physically:

____________________

____________________

What I ate today:

____________________

____________________

What I weighed today: ____________________

Daily "to-do's": *shopping/errands/home tasks/etc*

____________________

____________________

Memorable Headlines or Event of the Day: *(current event from the news or in my own life)*

____________________

____________________

**Baby Countdown: 10 weeks to go**

Due Date: ____________________

Week Thirty Date: ____________

## Daily Encouragement

*But now in Christ Jesus you who formerly were far off have been brought near by the blood of Christ. For He Himself is our peace.*

EPHESIANS 2:13-14 NASB

Appointments today: *Doctors/Dentist/Hair/Nails/etc.*

What I'm feeling in my heart and spirit:

What I'm feeling physically:

What I ate today:

What I weighed today: ____________

Daily "to-do's": *shopping/errands/home tasks/etc*

Memorable Headlines or Event of the Day: *(current event from the news or in my own life)*

**Baby Countdown: 10 weeks to go**

Due Date: ____________

WEEK THIRTY Date: ____________________

## DAILY ENCOURAGEMENT

*The greatest honor you can give Almighty God is to live gladly and joyfully because of the knowledge of His love.*

JULIANA OF NORWICH

Appointments today: *Doctors/Dentist/Hair/Nails/etc.*

_______________________________________________

_______________________________________________

What I'm feeling in my heart and spirit:

_______________________________________________

_______________________________________________

What I'm feeling physically:

_______________________________________________

_______________________________________________

What I ate today:

_______________________________________________

_______________________________________________

What I weighed today: ____________________________

Daily "to-do's": *shopping/errands/home tasks/etc*

_______________________________________________

_______________________________________________

Memorable Headlines or Event of the Day: *(current event from the news or in my own life)*

_______________________________________________

_______________________________________________

**Baby Countdown: 10 weeks to go**

Due Date: ____________________

WEEK THIRTY

## Personal Journal

YOU KNOW MY HEART LORD...

## A Mother's Prayer:

PRECIOUS BABY, I PRAY FOR YOU, I CARE FOR YOU, I LOVE YOU...

WEEK THIRTY-ONE Date: ____________________

## DAILY ENCOURAGEMENT

*Be strong and brave, and do the work. Don't be afraid or discouraged, because the Lord God, my God, is with you. He will not fail you or leave you.*

1 CHRONICLES 28:20 NCV

Appointments today: *Doctors/Dentist/Hair/Nails/etc.*

What I'm feeling in my heart and spirit:

What I'm feeling physically:

What I ate today:

What I weighed today: ____________________

Daily "to-do's": *shopping/errands/home tasks/etc*

Memorable Headlines or Event of the Day: *(current event from the news or in my own life)*

**Baby Countdown: 9 weeks to go**

Due Date: ____________________

## Week Thirty-One

*Date:* ______________________

### Daily Encouragement

*When we reach the end of our abilities, God's possibilities are just beginning.*

EMILIE BARNES

Appointments today: *Doctors/Dentist/Hair/Nails/etc.*

What I'm feeling in my heart and spirit:

What I'm feeling physically:

What I ate today:

What I weighed today: ______________________

Daily "to-do's": *shopping/errands/home tasks/etc*

Memorable Headlines or Event of the Day: *(current event from the news or in my own life)*

**Baby Countdown: 9 weeks to go**

Due Date: ______________________

WEEK THIRTY-ONE Date: ____________________

## DAILY ENCOURAGEMENT

*Let the hearts of those who seek the Lord rejoice. Look to the Lord and his strength; seek his face always.*

1 CHRONICLES 16:10–11 NIV

Appointments today: *Doctors/Dentist/Hair/Nails/etc.*

____________________

____________________

What I'm feeling in my heart and spirit:

____________________

____________________

What I'm feeling physically:

____________________

____________________

What I ate today:

____________________

____________________

What I weighed today: ____________________

Daily "to-do's": *shopping/errands/home tasks/etc*

____________________

____________________

Memorable Headlines or Event of the Day: *(current event from the news or in my own life)*

____________________

____________________

**Baby Countdown: 9 weeks to go**

Due Date: ____________________

## Week Thirty-One

*Date:* ______________________

### Daily Encouragement

*For whatever life holds for you and your family in the coming days, weave the unfailing fabric of God's Word through your heart and mind. It will hold strong.*

GIGI GRAHAM TCHIVIDJIAN

Appointments today: *Doctors/Dentist/Hair/Nails/etc.*

______________________

______________________

What I'm feeling in my heart and spirit:

______________________

______________________

What I'm feeling physically:

______________________

______________________

What I ate today:

______________________

______________________

What I weighed today: ______________________

Daily "to-do's": *shopping/errands/home tasks/etc*

______________________

______________________

Memorable Headlines or Event of the Day: *(current event from the news or in my own life)*

______________________

______________________

**Baby Countdown: 9 weeks to go**

Due Date: ______________________

Week Thirty-One Date: ____________

## Daily Encouragement

*Trust in the LORD with all your heart; do not depend on your own understanding.*

PROVERBS 3:5 NLT

Appointments today: *Doctors/Dentist/Hair/Nails/etc.*

____________

____________

What I'm feeling in my heart and spirit:

____________

____________

What I'm feeling physically:

____________

____________

What I ate today:

____________

____________

What I weighed today: ____________

Daily "to-do's": *shopping/errands/home tasks/etc*

____________

____________

Memorable Headlines or Event of the Day: *(current event from the news or in my own life)*

____________

____________

**Baby Countdown: 9 weeks to go**

Due Date: ____________

Week Thirty-One

## *Personal Journal*

You know my heart Lord...

## *A Mother's Prayer:*

Precious baby, I pray for you, I care for you, I love you...

WEEK THIRTY-TWO Date: ____________________

## DAILY ENCOURAGEMENT

*When we reach the end of our strength, wisdom, and personal resources, we enter into the beginning of his glorious provisions.*

PATSY CLAIRMONT

Appointments today: *Doctors/Dentist/Hair/Nails/etc.*

______________________________________________

______________________________________________

What I'm feeling in my heart and spirit:

______________________________________________

______________________________________________

What I'm feeling physically:

______________________________________________

______________________________________________

What I ate today:

______________________________________________

______________________________________________

What I weighed today: ____________________

Daily "to-do's": *shopping/errands/home tasks/etc*

______________________________________________

______________________________________________

Memorable Headlines or Event of the Day: *(current event from the news or in my own life)*

______________________________________________

______________________________________________

**Baby Countdown: 8 weeks to go**

Due Date: ____________________

Week Thirty-Two    *Date:* ______________________

## Daily Encouragement

*The Lord will work out his plans for my life—for your faithful love, O Lord, endures forever.*

PSALM 138:8 NLT

Appointments today: *Doctors/Dentist/Hair/Nails/etc.*

______________________

______________________

What I'm feeling in my heart and spirit:

______________________

______________________

What I'm feeling physically:

______________________

______________________

What I ate today:

______________________

______________________

What I weighed today: ______________________

Daily "to-do's": *shopping/errands/home tasks/etc*

______________________

______________________

Memorable Headlines or Event of the Day: *(current event from the news or in my own life)*

______________________

______________________

**Baby Countdown: 8 weeks to go**

Due Date: ______________________

WEEK THIRTY-TWO    *Date:* ______________________

## DAILY ENCOURAGEMENT

*God has no problems, only plans. There is never panic in heaven.*

CORRIE TEN BOOM

Appointments today: *Doctors/Dentist/Hair/Nails/etc.*

______________________________________________

______________________________________________

What I'm feeling in my heart and spirit:

______________________________________________

______________________________________________

What I'm feeling physically:

______________________________________________

______________________________________________

What I ate today:

______________________________________________

______________________________________________

What I weighed today: ______________________

Daily "to-do's": *shopping/errands/home tasks/etc*

______________________________________________

______________________________________________

Memorable Headlines or Event of the Day: *(current event from the news or in my own life)*

______________________________________________

______________________________________________

**Baby Countdown: 8 weeks to go**

Due Date: ______________________

WEEK THIRTY-TWO Date: ______________________

## DAILY ENCOURAGEMENT

*The LORD will give strength to His people; The LORD will bless His people with peace.*

PSALM 29:11 NKJV

Appointments today: *Doctors/Dentist/Hair/Nails/etc.*

______________________

______________________

What I'm feeling in my heart and spirit:

______________________

______________________

What I'm feeling physically:

______________________

______________________

What I ate today:

______________________

______________________

What I weighed today: ______________________

Daily "to-do's": *shopping/errands/home tasks/etc*

______________________

______________________

Memorable Headlines or Event of the Day: *(current event from the news or in my own life)*

______________________

______________________

**Baby Countdown: 8 weeks to go**

Due Date: ______________________

WEEK THIRTY-TWO Date: ____________________

## DAILY ENCOURAGEMENT

*Those who are God's without reserve are, in every sense, content.*

HANNAH WHITALL SMITH

Appointments today: *Doctors/Dentist/Hair/Nails/etc.*

______________________________

______________________________

What I'm feeling in my heart and spirit:

______________________________

______________________________

What I'm feeling physically:

______________________________

______________________________

What I ate today:

______________________________

______________________________

What I weighed today: ____________________

Daily "to-do's": *shopping/errands/home tasks/etc*

______________________________

______________________________

Memorable Headlines or Event of the Day: *(current event from the news or in my own life)*

______________________________

______________________________

**Baby Countdown: 8 weeks to go**

Due Date: ____________________

Week Thirty-Two

## *Personal Journal*

You know my heart Lord...

## *A Mother's Prayer:*

Precious baby, I pray for you, I care for you, I love you...

WEEK THIRTY-THREE    *Date:* ____________________

## DAILY ENCOURAGEMENT

*The Lord is my shepherd; I shall not want.*

PSALM 23:1 KJV

Appointments today: *Doctors/Dentist/Hair/Nails/etc.*

______________________________

______________________________

What I'm feeling in my heart and spirit:

______________________________

______________________________

What I'm feeling physically:

______________________________

______________________________

What I ate today:

______________________________

______________________________

What I weighed today: ____________________

Daily "to-do's": *shopping/errands/home tasks/etc*

______________________________

______________________________

Memorable Headlines or Event of the Day: *(current event from the news or in my own life)*

______________________________

______________________________

**Baby Countdown: 7 weeks to go**

Due Date: ____________________

## Week Thirty-Three

*Date:* ______________________

### Daily Encouragement

*God loves you and wants you to experience peace and life—abundant and eternal.*

BILLY GRAHAM

Appointments today: *Doctors/Dentist/Hair/Nails/etc.*

What I'm feeling in my heart and spirit:

What I'm feeling physically:

What I ate today:

What I weighed today: ______________________

Daily "to-do's": *shopping/errands/home tasks/etc*

Memorable Headlines or Event of the Day: *(current event from the news or in my own life)*

**Baby Countdown: 7 weeks to go**

Due Date: ______________________

WEEK THIRTY-THREE Date: ____________________

## DAILY ENCOURAGEMENT

*Come unto me, all ye that labor and are heavy laden, and I will give you rest.*

MATTHEW 11:28 KJV

Appointments today: *Doctors/Dentist/Hair/Nails/etc.*

______________________________________________

______________________________________________

What I'm feeling in my heart and spirit:

______________________________________________

______________________________________________

What I'm feeling physically:

______________________________________________

______________________________________________

What I ate today:

______________________________________________

______________________________________________

What I weighed today: ______________________________

Daily "to-do's": *shopping/errands/home tasks/etc*

______________________________________________

______________________________________________

Memorable Headlines or Event of the Day: *(current event from the news or in my own life)*

______________________________________________

______________________________________________

**Baby Countdown: 7 weeks to go**

Due Date: ____________________

## Week Thirty-Three Date: ____________

### Daily Encouragement

*Life is strenuous. See that your clock does not run down.*

MRS. CHARLES E. COWMAN

Appointments today: *Doctors/Dentist/Hair/Nails/etc.*

______________________________

______________________________

What I'm feeling in my heart and spirit:

______________________________

______________________________

What I'm feeling physically:

______________________________

______________________________

What I ate today:

______________________________

______________________________

What I weighed today: ____________

Daily "to-do's": *shopping/errands/home tasks/etc*

______________________________

______________________________

Memorable Headlines or Event of the Day: *(current event from the news or in my own life)*

______________________________

______________________________

**Baby Countdown: 7 weeks to go**

Due Date: ____________

## WEEK THIRTY-THREE

*Date:* ____________________

### DAILY ENCOURAGEMENT

*Now the just shall live by faith.*

HEBREWS 10:38 NKJV

Appointments today: *Doctors/Dentist/Hair/Nails/etc.*

What I'm feeling in my heart and spirit:

What I'm feeling physically:

What I ate today:

What I weighed today: ____________________

Daily "to-do's": *shopping/errands/home tasks/etc*

Memorable Headlines or Event of the Day: *(current event from the news or in my own life)*

**Baby Countdown: 7 weeks to go**

Due Date: ____________________

Week Thirty-Three

## *Personal Journal*

You know my heart Lord...

## *A Mother's Prayer:*

Precious baby, I pray for you, I care for you, I love you...

WEEK THIRTY-FOUR Date: ____________________

## DAILY ENCOURAGEMENT

*Let me encourage you to continue to wait with faith. God may not perform a miracle, but He is trustworthy to touch you and make you whole.*

LISA WHELCHEL

Appointments today: *Doctors/Dentist/Hair/Nails/etc.*

______________________________________________

______________________________________________

What I'm feeling in my heart and spirit:

______________________________________________

______________________________________________

What I'm feeling physically:

______________________________________________

______________________________________________

What I ate today:

______________________________________________

______________________________________________

What I weighed today: ______________________

Daily "to-do's": *shopping/errands/home tasks/etc*

______________________________________________

______________________________________________

Memorable Headlines or Event of the Day: *(current event from the news or in my own life)*

______________________________________________

______________________________________________

**Baby Countdown: 6 weeks to go**

Due Date: ____________________

Week Thirty-Four Date: ______________________

## Daily Encouragement

*Praise the Lord, all nations! Glorify Him, all peoples! For great is His faithful love to us; the Lord's faithfulness endures forever. Hallelujah!*

PSALM 117 HCSB

Appointments today: *Doctors/Dentist/Hair/Nails/etc.*

______________________

______________________

What I'm feeling in my heart and spirit:

______________________

______________________

What I'm feeling physically:

______________________

______________________

What I ate today:

______________________

______________________

What I weighed today: ______________________

Daily "to-do's": *shopping/errands/home tasks/etc*

______________________

______________________

Memorable Headlines or Event of the Day: *(current event from the news or in my own life)*

______________________

______________________

**Baby Countdown: 6 weeks to go**

Due Date: ______________________

WEEK THIRTY-FOUR Date: ____________________

## DAILY ENCOURAGEMENT

*Though our feelings come and go, His love for us does not.*

C. S. LEWIS

Appointments today: *Doctors/Dentist/Hair/Nails/etc.*

________________________________________

________________________________________

What I'm feeling in my heart and spirit:

________________________________________

________________________________________

What I'm feeling physically:

________________________________________

________________________________________

What I ate today:

________________________________________

________________________________________

What I weighed today: ____________________

Daily "to-do's": *shopping/errands/home tasks/etc*

________________________________________

________________________________________

Memorable Headlines or Event of the Day: *(current event from the news or in my own life)*

________________________________________

________________________________________

**Baby Countdown: 6 weeks to go**

Due Date: ____________________

Week Thirty-Four *Date:* ______________________

## Daily Encouragement

*Is anyone happy? Let him sing songs of praise.*

JAMES 5:13 NIV

Appointments today: *Doctors/Dentist/Hair/Nails/etc.*

______________________

______________________

What I'm feeling in my heart and spirit:

______________________

______________________

What I'm feeling physically:

______________________

______________________

What I ate today:

______________________

______________________

What I weighed today: ______________________

Daily "to-do's": *shopping/errands/home tasks/etc*

______________________

______________________

Memorable Headlines or Event of the Day: *(current event from the news or in my own life)*

______________________

______________________

**Baby Countdown: 6 weeks to go**

Due Date: ______________________

## Week Thirty-Four

*Date:* ______________________

### Daily Encouragement

*Our God is the sovereign Creator of the universe! He loves us as His own children and has provided every good thing we have; He is worthy of our praise every moment.*

SHIRLEY DOBSON

Appointments today: *Doctors/Dentist/Hair/Nails/etc.*

______________________

______________________

What I'm feeling in my heart and spirit:

______________________

______________________

What I'm feeling physically:

______________________

______________________

What I ate today:

______________________

______________________

What I weighed today: ______________________

Daily "to-do's": *shopping/errands/home tasks/etc*

______________________

______________________

Memorable Headlines or Event of the Day: *(current event from the news or in my own life)*

______________________

______________________

**Baby Countdown: 6 weeks to go**

Due Date: ______________________

WEEK THIRTY-FOUR

## *Personal Journal*

YOU KNOW MY HEART LORD...

## *A Mother's Prayer:*

PRECIOUS BABY, I PRAY FOR YOU, I CARE FOR YOU, I LOVE YOU...

Week Thirty-Five Date: ______________________

## Daily Encouragement

*The earnest prayer of a righteous person has great power and wonderful results.*

JAMES 5:16 NLT

Appointments today: *Doctors/Dentist/Hair/Nails/etc.*

______________________

______________________

What I'm feeling in my heart and spirit:

______________________

______________________

What I'm feeling physically:

______________________

______________________

What I ate today:

______________________

______________________

What I weighed today: ______________________

Daily "to-do's": *shopping/errands/home tasks/etc*

______________________

______________________

Memorable Headlines or Event of the Day: *(current event from the news or in my own life)*

______________________

______________________

**Baby Countdown: 5 weeks to go**

Due Date: ______________________

WEEK THIRTY-FIVE Date: ____________________

## DAILY ENCOURAGEMENT

*Prayer moves the arm that moves the world.*

ANNIE ARMSTRONG

Appointments today: *Doctors/Dentist/Hair/Nails/etc.*

_______________________________________________

_______________________________________________

What I'm feeling in my heart and spirit:

_______________________________________________

_______________________________________________

What I'm feeling physically:

_______________________________________________

_______________________________________________

What I ate today:

_______________________________________________

_______________________________________________

What I weighed today: ____________________

Daily "to-do's": *shopping/errands/home tasks/etc*

_______________________________________________

_______________________________________________

Memorable Headlines or Event of the Day: *(current event from the news or in my own life)*

_______________________________________________

_______________________________________________

**Baby Countdown: 5 weeks to go**

Due Date: ____________________

WEEK THIRTY-FIVE Date: ___________________

## DAILY ENCOURAGEMENT

*A word spoken at the right time is like golden apples on a silver tray.*

PROVERBS 25:11 HCSB

Appointments today: *Doctors/Dentist/Hair/Nails/etc.*

---

---

What I'm feeling in my heart and spirit:

---

---

What I'm feeling physically:

---

---

What I ate today:

---

---

What I weighed today: ___________________

Daily "to-do's": *shopping/errands/home tasks/etc*

---

---

Memorable Headlines or Event of the Day: *(current event from the news or in my own life)*

---

---

**Baby Countdown: 5 weeks to go**

Due Date: ___________________

WEEK THIRTY-FIVE Date: ______________________

## DAILY ENCOURAGEMENT

*Always stay connected to people and seek out things that bring you joy. Dream with abandon. Pray confidently.*

BARBARA JOHNSON

Appointments today: *Doctors/Dentist/Hair/Nails/etc.*

______________________

______________________

What I'm feeling in my heart and spirit:

______________________

______________________

What I'm feeling physically:

______________________

______________________

What I ate today:

______________________

______________________

What I weighed today: ______________________

Daily "to-do's": *shopping/errands/home tasks/etc*

______________________

______________________

Memorable Headlines or Event of the Day: *(current event from the news or in my own life)*

______________________

______________________

**Baby Countdown: 5 weeks to go**

Due Date: ______________________

Week Thirty-Five Date: ____________________

## Daily Encouragement

*But seek first his kingdom and his righteousness, and all these things will be given to you as well. Therefore do not worry about tomorrow, for tomorrow will worry about itself. Each day has enough trouble of its own.*

MATTHEW 6:33-34 NIV

Appointments today: *Doctors/Dentist/Hair/Nails/etc.*

________________________________________

________________________________________

What I'm feeling in my heart and spirit:

________________________________________

________________________________________

What I'm feeling physically:

________________________________________

________________________________________

What I ate today:

________________________________________

________________________________________

What I weighed today: ____________________

Daily "to-do's": *shopping/errands/home tasks/etc*

________________________________________

________________________________________

Memorable Headlines or Event of the Day: *(current event from the news or in my own life)*

________________________________________

________________________________________

**Baby Countdown: 5 weeks to go**

Due Date: ____________________

Week Thirty-Five

## Personal Journal

You know my heart Lord...

## A Mother's Prayer:

Precious baby, I pray for you, I care for you, I love you...

Week Thirty-Six Date: ______________________

## Daily Encouragement

*Today is mine. Tomorrow is none of my business. If I peer anxiously into the fog of the future, I will strain my spiritual eyes so that I will not see clearly what is required of me now.*

ELISABETH ELLIOTT

Appointments today: *Doctors/Dentist/Hair/Nails/etc.*

______________________

______________________

What I'm feeling in my heart and spirit:

______________________

______________________

What I'm feeling physically:

______________________

______________________

What I ate today:

______________________

______________________

What I weighed today: ______________________

Daily "to-do's": *shopping/errands/home tasks/etc*

______________________

______________________

Memorable Headlines or Event of the Day: *(current event from the news or in my own life)*

______________________

______________________

**Baby Countdown: 4 weeks to go**

Due Date: ______________________

## Week Thirty-Six

*Date:* ______________________

### Daily Encouragement

*And when the woman saw that she was not hid, she came trembling, and falling down before him, she declared unto him before all the people for what cause she had touched him, and how she was healed immediately. And he said unto her, Daughter, be of good comfort: thy faith hath made thee whole; go in peace.*

LUKE 8:47-48 KJV

Appointments today: *Doctors/Dentist/Hair/Nails/etc.*

______________________

______________________

What I'm feeling in my heart and spirit:

______________________

______________________

What I'm feeling physically:

______________________

______________________

What I ate today:

______________________

______________________

What I weighed today: ______________________

Daily "to-do's": *shopping/errands/home tasks/etc*

______________________

______________________

Memorable Headlines or Event of the Day: *(current event from the news or in my own life)*

______________________

______________________

**Baby Countdown: 4 weeks to go**

Due Date: ______________________

Week Thirty-Six Date: ____________

## Daily Encouragement

*The more closely you cling to the Lord Jesus, the more clear will your peace be.*

C. H. SPURGEON

Appointments today: *Doctors/Dentist/Hair/Nails/etc.*

What I'm feeling in my heart and spirit:

What I'm feeling physically:

What I ate today:

What I weighed today: ____________

Daily "to-do's": *shopping/errands/home tasks/etc*

Memorable Headlines or Event of the Day: *(current event from the news or in my own life)*

**Baby Countdown: 4 weeks to go**

Due Date: ____________

WEEK THIRTY-SIX Date: ______________________

## DAILY ENCOURAGEMENT

*Cast thy burden upon the LORD, and he shall sustain thee: he shall never suffer the righteous to be moved.*

PSALM 55:22 KJV

Appointments today: *Doctors/Dentist/Hair/Nails/etc.*

______________________

______________________

What I'm feeling in my heart and spirit:

______________________

______________________

What I'm feeling physically:

______________________

______________________

What I ate today:

______________________

______________________

What I weighed today: ______________________

Daily "to-do's": *shopping/errands/home tasks/etc*

______________________

______________________

Memorable Headlines or Event of the Day: *(current event from the news or in my own life)*

______________________

______________________

**Baby Countdown: 4 weeks to go**

Due Date: ______________________

## Week Thirty-Six

*Date:* ______________________

### Daily Encouragement

*To yield to God means to belong to God, and to belong to God means to have all His infinite power. To belong to God means to have all.*

HANNAH WHITALL SMITH

Appointments today: *Doctors/Dentist/Hair/Nails/etc.*

______________________

______________________

What I'm feeling in my heart and spirit:

______________________

______________________

What I'm feeling physically:

______________________

______________________

What I ate today:

______________________

______________________

What I weighed today: ______________________

Daily "to-do's": *shopping/errands/home tasks/etc*

______________________

______________________

Memorable Headlines or Event of the Day: *(current event from the news or in my own life)*

______________________

______________________

**Baby Countdown: 4 weeks to go**

Due Date: ______________________

WEEK THIRTY-SIX

## Personal Journal

YOU KNOW MY HEART LORD...

## A Mother's Prayer:

PRECIOUS BABY, I PRAY FOR YOU, I CARE FOR YOU, I LOVE YOU...

Week Thirty-Seven Date: ______________________

## Daily Encouragement

*I have come that they may have life, and that they may have it more abundantly.*

JOHN 10:10 NKJV

Appointments today: *Doctors/Dentist/Hair/Nails/etc.*

______________________

______________________

What I'm feeling in my heart and spirit:

______________________

______________________

What I'm feeling physically:

______________________

______________________

What I ate today:

______________________

______________________

What I weighed today: ______________________

Daily "to-do's": *shopping/errands/home tasks/etc*

______________________

______________________

Memorable Headlines or Event of the Day: *(current event from the news or in my own life)*

______________________

______________________

**Baby Countdown: 3 weeks to go**

Due Date: ______________________

WEEK THIRTY-SEVEN Date: ____________________

## DAILY ENCOURAGEMENT

*If you want purpose and meaning and satisfaction and fulfillment and peace and hope and joy and abundant life that lasts forever, look to Jesus.*

ANNE GRAHAM LOTZ

Appointments today: *Doctors/Dentist/Hair/Nails/etc.*

What I'm feeling in my heart and spirit:

What I'm feeling physically:

What I ate today:

What I weighed today: ____________________

Daily "to-do's": *shopping/errands/home tasks/etc*

Memorable Headlines or Event of the Day: *(current event from the news or in my own life)*

**Baby Countdown: 3 weeks to go**

Due Date: ____________________

## Week Thirty-Seven

Date: ____________________

### Daily Encouragement

*Careful planning puts you ahead in the long run; hurry and scurry puts you further behind.*

PROVERBS 21:5 MSG

Appointments today: *Doctors/Dentist/Hair/Nails/etc.*

____________________

____________________

What I'm feeling in my heart and spirit:

____________________

____________________

What I'm feeling physically:

____________________

____________________

What I ate today:

____________________

____________________

What I weighed today: ____________________

Daily "to-do's": *shopping/errands/home tasks/etc*

____________________

____________________

Memorable Headlines or Event of the Day: *(current event from the news or in my own life)*

____________________

____________________

**Baby Countdown: 3 weeks to go**

Due Date: ____________________

## Week Thirty-Seven

*Date:* ______________________

### Daily Encouragement

*A #2 pencil and a dream can take you anywhere.*

JOYCE MEYER

Appointments today: *Doctors/Dentist/Hair/Nails/etc.*

______________________

______________________

What I'm feeling in my heart and spirit:

______________________

______________________

What I'm feeling physically:

______________________

______________________

What I ate today:

______________________

______________________

What I weighed today: ______________________

Daily "to-do's": *shopping/errands/home tasks/etc*

______________________

______________________

Memorable Headlines or Event of the Day: *(current event from the news or in my own life)*

______________________

______________________

**Baby Countdown: 3 weeks to go**

Due Date: ______________________

Week Thirty-Seven Date: ____________________

## Daily Encouragement

*I sought the Lord, and He answered me and delivered me from all my fears.*

PSALM 34:4 HCSB

Appointments today: *Doctors/Dentist/Hair/Nails/etc.*

______________________________

______________________________

What I'm feeling in my heart and spirit:

______________________________

______________________________

What I'm feeling physically:

______________________________

______________________________

What I ate today:

______________________________

______________________________

What I weighed today: ____________________

Daily "to-do's": *shopping/errands/home tasks/etc*

______________________________

______________________________

Memorable Headlines or Event of the Day: *(current event from the news or in my own life)*

______________________________

______________________________

**Baby Countdown: 3 weeks to go**

Due Date: ____________________

Week Thirty-Seven

## Personal Journal

You know my heart Lord...

## A Mother's Prayer:

Precious baby, I pray for you, I care for you, I love you...

Week Thirty-Eight Date: ______________

Daily Encouragement

*Do not build up obstacles in your imagination. Difficulties must be studied and dealt with, but they must not be magnified by fear.*

NORMAN VINCENT PEALE

Appointments today: *Doctors/Dentist/Hair/Nails/etc.*

What I'm feeling in my heart and spirit:

What I'm feeling physically:

What I ate today:

What I weighed today: ______________

Daily "to-do's": *shopping/errands/home tasks/etc*

Memorable Headlines or Event of the Day: *(current event from the news or in my own life)*

**Baby Countdown: 2 weeks to go**

Due Date: ______________

## Week Thirty-Eight

*Date:* ______________________

### Daily Encouragement

*Therefore, since we are receiving a kingdom that cannot be shaken, let us hold on to grace. By it, we may serve God acceptably, with reverence and awe.*

HEBREWS 12:28 HCSB

Appointments today: *Doctors/Dentist/Hair/Nails/etc.*

______________________

______________________

What I'm feeling in my heart and spirit:

______________________

______________________

What I'm feeling physically:

______________________

______________________

What I ate today:

______________________

______________________

What I weighed today: ______________________

Daily "to-do's": *shopping/errands/home tasks/etc*

______________________

______________________

Memorable Headlines or Event of the Day: *(current event from the news or in my own life)*

______________________

______________________

**Baby Countdown: 2 weeks to go**

Due Date: ______________________

WEEK THIRTY-EIGHT Date: ____________________

## DAILY ENCOURAGEMENT

*If our hearts have been attuned to God through an abiding faith in Christ, the result will be joyous optimism and good cheer.*

BILLY GRAHAM

Appointments today: *Doctors/Dentist/Hair/Nails/etc.*

_______________________________________________

_______________________________________________

What I'm feeling in my heart and spirit:

_______________________________________________

_______________________________________________

What I'm feeling physically:

_______________________________________________

_______________________________________________

What I ate today:

_______________________________________________

_______________________________________________

What I weighed today: ____________________

Daily "to-do's": *shopping/errands/home tasks/etc*

_______________________________________________

_______________________________________________

Memorable Headlines or Event of the Day: *(current event from the news or in my own life)*

_______________________________________________

_______________________________________________

**Baby Countdown: 2 weeks to go**

Due Date: ____________________

## Week Thirty-Eight

Date: ____________________

### Daily Encouragement

*We always thank God, the Father of our Lord Jesus Christ.*

COLOSSIANS 1:3 NCV

Appointments today: *Doctors/Dentist/Hair/Nails/etc.*

______________________________

______________________________

What I'm feeling in my heart and spirit:

______________________________

______________________________

What I'm feeling physically:

______________________________

______________________________

What I ate today:

______________________________

______________________________

What I weighed today: ____________________

Daily "to-do's": *shopping/errands/home tasks/etc*

______________________________

______________________________

Memorable Headlines or Event of the Day: *(current event from the news or in my own life)*

______________________________

______________________________

**Baby Countdown: 2 weeks to go**

Due Date: ____________________

## Week Thirty-Eight

*Date:* ____________________

### Daily Encouragement

*Christ is the secret, the source, the substance, the center, and the circumference of all true and lasting gladness.*

MRS. CHARLES E. COWMAN

Appointments today: *Doctors/Dentist/Hair/Nails/etc.*

What I'm feeling in my heart and spirit:

What I'm feeling physically:

What I ate today:

What I weighed today: ____________________

Daily "to-do's": *shopping/errands/home tasks/etc*

Memorable Headlines or Event of the Day: *(current event from the news or in my own life)*

**Baby Countdown: 2 weeks to go**

Due Date: ____________________

Week Thirty-Eight

## Personal Journal

You know my heart Lord…

## A Mother's Prayer:

Precious baby, I pray for you, I care for you, I love you…

WEEK THIRTY-NINE Date: ____________________

## DAILY ENCOURAGEMENT

*For God so loved the world that He gave His only begotten Son, that whoever believes in Him should not perish but have everlasting life.*

JOHN 3:16 NKJV

Appointments today: *Doctors/Dentist/Hair/Nails/etc.*

______________________________

______________________________

What I'm feeling in my heart and spirit:

______________________________

______________________________

What I'm feeling physically:

______________________________

______________________________

What I ate today:

______________________________

______________________________

What I weighed today: ____________________

Daily "to-do's": *shopping/errands/home tasks/etc*

______________________________

______________________________

Memorable Headlines or Event of the Day: *(current event from the news or in my own life)*

______________________________

______________________________

**Baby Countdown: 1 week to go**

Due Date: ____________________

WEEK THIRTY-NINE Date: ______________________

## DAILY ENCOURAGEMENT

*Let us see the victorious Jesus, the conqueror of the tomb, the one who defied death. And let us be reminded that we, too, will be granted the same victory.*

MAX LUCADO

Appointments today: *Doctors/Dentist/Hair/Nails/etc.*

______________________

______________________

What I'm feeling in my heart and spirit:

______________________

______________________

What I'm feeling physically:

______________________

______________________

What I ate today:

______________________

______________________

What I weighed today: ______________________

Daily "to-do's": *shopping/errands/home tasks/etc*

______________________

______________________

Memorable Headlines or Event of the Day: *(current event from the news or in my own life)*

______________________

______________________

**Baby Countdown: 1 week to go**

Due Date: ______________________

Week Thirty-Nine Date: ______________________

## Daily Encouragement

*He put a child in the middle of the room. Then, cradling the little one in his arms, he said, "Whoever embraces one of these children as I do embraces me, and far more than me—God who sent me."*

MARK 9:36-37 MSG

Appointments today: *Doctors/Dentist/Hair/Nails/etc.*

______________________________________________

______________________________________________

What I'm feeling in my heart and spirit:

______________________________________________

______________________________________________

What I'm feeling physically:

______________________________________________

______________________________________________

What I ate today:

______________________________________________

______________________________________________

What I weighed today: ______________________

Daily "to-do's": *shopping/errands/home tasks/etc*

______________________________________________

______________________________________________

Memorable Headlines or Event of the Day: *(current event from the news or in my own life)*

______________________________________________

______________________________________________

**Baby Countdown: 1 week to go**

Due Date: ______________________

WEEK THIRTY-NINE Date: ______________

## DAILY ENCOURAGEMENT

*There is no more influential or powerful role on earth than a mother's.*

CHARLES SWINDOLL

Appointments today: *Doctors/Dentist/Hair/Nails/etc.*

______________________________

______________________________

What I'm feeling in my heart and spirit:

______________________________

______________________________

What I'm feeling physically:

______________________________

______________________________

What I ate today:

______________________________

______________________________

What I weighed today: ______________

Daily "to-do's": *shopping/errands/home tasks/etc*

______________________________

______________________________

Memorable Headlines or Event of the Day: *(current event from the news or in my own life)*

______________________________

______________________________

**Baby Countdown: 1 week to go**

Due Date: ______________

Week Thirty-Nine  *Date:* ______________________

Daily Encouragement

*Her children rise up and call her blessed.*

PROVERBS 31:28 NKJV

Appointments today: *Doctors/Dentist/Hair/Nails/etc.*

______________________

______________________

What I'm feeling in my heart and spirit:

______________________

______________________

What I'm feeling physically:

______________________

______________________

What I ate today:

______________________

______________________

What I weighed today: ______________________

Daily "to-do's": *shopping/errands/home tasks/etc*

______________________

______________________

Memorable Headlines or Event of the Day: *(current event from the news or in my own life)*

______________________

______________________

**Baby Countdown: 1 week to go**

Due Date: ______________________

Week Thirty-Nine

## *Personal Journal*

You know my heart Lord…

## *A Mother's Prayer:*

Precious baby, I pray for you, I care for you, I love you…

WEEK FORTY Date: ______________

DAILY ENCOURAGEMENT

*The woman is the heart of the home.*

MOTHER TERESA

Appointments today: *Doctors/Dentist/Hair/Nails/etc.*

______________

______________

What I'm feeling in my heart and spirit:

______________

______________

What I'm feeling physically:

______________

______________

What I ate today:

______________

______________

What I weighed today: ______________

Daily "to-do's": *shopping/errands/home tasks/etc*

______________

______________

Memorable Headlines or Event of the Day: *(current event from the news or in my own life)*

______________

______________

**Baby Countdown: any day now!**

Due Date: ______________

Week Forty    *Date:* ______________________

## Daily Encouragement

*Let the words of my mouth and the meditation of my heart be acceptable in Your sight, O Lord, my strength and my Redeemer.*

PSALM 19:14 NKJV

Appointments today: *Doctors/Dentist/Hair/Nails/etc.*

______________________

______________________

What I'm feeling in my heart and spirit:

______________________

______________________

What I'm feeling physically:

______________________

______________________

What I ate today:

______________________

______________________

What I weighed today: ______________________

Daily "to-do's": *shopping/errands/home tasks/etc*

______________________

______________________

Memorable Headlines or Event of the Day: *(current event from the news or in my own life)*

______________________

______________________

**Baby Countdown: any day now!**

Due Date: ______________________

WEEK FORTY Date: ____________________

## DAILY ENCOURAGEMENT

*A person who has a praying mother has a most cherished possession.*

BILLY GRAHAM

Appointments today: *Doctors/Dentist/Hair/Nails/etc.*

______________________________

______________________________

What I'm feeling in my heart and spirit:

______________________________

______________________________

What I'm feeling physically:

______________________________

______________________________

What I ate today:

______________________________

______________________________

What I weighed today: ____________________

Daily "to-do's": *shopping/errands/home tasks/etc*

______________________________

______________________________

Memorable Headlines or Event of the Day: *(current event from the news or in my own life)*

______________________________

______________________________

**Baby Countdown: any day now!**

Due Date: ____________________

Week Forty Date: ______________________

## Daily Encouragement

*Thanks be to God for His indescribable gift.*

2 CORINTHIANS 9:15 HCSB

Appointments today: *Doctors/Dentist/Hair/Nails/etc.*

What I'm feeling in my heart and spirit:

What I'm feeling physically:

What I ate today:

What I weighed today: ______________________

Daily "to-do's": *shopping/errands/home tasks/etc*

Memorable Headlines or Event of the Day: *(current event from the news or in my own life)*

**Baby Countdown: any day now!**

Due Date: ______________________

WEEK FORTY Date: ____________________

## DAILY ENCOURAGEMENT

*Not every day of our lives is overflowing with joy and celebration. But there are moments when our hearts nearly burst within us for the sheer joy of being alive. The first sight of our newborn babies, the warmth of love in another's eyes . . . moments like these renew in us a heartfelt appreciation for life.*

GWEN ELLIS

Appointments today: *Doctors/Dentist/Hair/Nails/etc.*

______________________________

______________________________

What I'm feeling in my heart and spirit:

______________________________

______________________________

What I'm feeling physically:

______________________________

______________________________

What I ate today:

______________________________

______________________________

What I weighed today: ____________________

Daily "to-do's": *shopping/errands/home tasks/etc*

______________________________

______________________________

Memorable Headlines or Event of the Day: *(current event from the news or in my own life)*

______________________________

______________________________

**Baby Countdown: any day now!**

Due Date: ____________________

Week Forty

## Personal Journal

You know my heart Lord…

## A Mother's Prayer:

Precious baby, I pray for you, I care for you, I love you…

# Physician's Appointments

Date: ____________________

Time: ____________________

Doctors Name and Address: ____________________

Phone Number: __________ Fax Number: __________

Reason for Visit: ____________________

Questions to Ask: ____________________

Answers: ____________________

Concerns? ____________________

Date: ____________________

Time: ____________________

Doctors Name and Address: ____________________

Phone Number: __________ Fax Number: __________

Reason for Visit: ____________________

Questions to Ask: ____________________

Answers: ____________________

Concerns? ____________________

*Lord, watch over me and my precious little one. I trust you and your loving arms to always be around us!*

# *Physician's Appointments*

Date: ________________________________________

Time: ________________________________________

Doctors Name and Address: ____________________________

Phone Number: __________________ Fax Number: __________________

Reason for Visit: __________________________________

Questions to Ask: __________________________________

______________________________________________

Answers: ________________________________________

______________________________________________

Concerns? ________________________________________

______________________________________________

Date: ________________________________________

Time: ________________________________________

Doctors Name and Address: ____________________________

Phone Number: __________________ Fax Number: __________________

Reason for Visit: __________________________________

Questions to Ask: __________________________________

______________________________________________

Answers: ________________________________________

______________________________________________

Concerns? ________________________________________

______________________________________________

*Lord, watch over me and my precious little one. I trust you and your loving arms to always be around us!*

# Physician's Appointments

Date: ______________________

Time: ______________________

Doctors Name and Address: ______________________

Phone Number: ______________ Fax Number: ______________

Reason for Visit: ______________________

Questions to Ask: ______________________

______________________

Answers: ______________________

______________________

Concerns? ______________________

______________________

Date: ______________________

Time: ______________________

Doctors Name and Address: ______________________

Phone Number: ______________ Fax Number: ______________

Reason for Visit: ______________________

Questions to Ask: ______________________

______________________

Answers: ______________________

______________________

Concerns? ______________________

______________________

*Lord, watch over me and my precious little one. I trust you and your loving arms to always be around us!*

# Physician's Appointments

Date: ______________________________

Time: ______________________________

Doctors Name and Address: ______________________________

Phone Number: ______________ Fax Number: ______________

Reason for Visit: ______________________________

Questions to Ask: ______________________________

______________________________

Answers: ______________________________

______________________________

Concerns? ______________________________

______________________________

Date: ______________________________

Time: ______________________________

Doctors Name and Address: ______________________________

Phone Number: ______________ Fax Number: ______________

Reason for Visit: ______________________________

Questions to Ask: ______________________________

______________________________

Answers: ______________________________

______________________________

Concerns? ______________________________

______________________________

*Lord, watch over me and my precious little one. I trust you and your loving arms to always be around us!*

# Physician's Appointments

Date: ____________________

Time: ____________________

Doctors Name and Address: ____________________

Phone Number: ____________________ Fax Number: ____________________

Reason for Visit: ____________________

Questions to Ask: ____________________

Answers: ____________________

Concerns? ____________________

Date: ____________________

Time: ____________________

Doctors Name and Address: ____________________

Phone Number: ____________________ Fax Number: ____________________

Reason for Visit: ____________________

Questions to Ask: ____________________

Answers: ____________________

Concerns? ____________________

*Lord, watch over me and my precious little one. I trust you and your loving arms to always be around us!*

# Physician's Appointments

Date: ____________________

Time: ____________________

Doctors Name and Address: ____________________

Phone Number: ____________________ Fax Number: ____________________

Reason for Visit: ____________________

Questions to Ask: ____________________

____________________

Answers: ____________________

____________________

Concerns? ____________________

____________________

Date: ____________________

Time: ____________________

Doctors Name and Address: ____________________

Phone Number: ____________________ Fax Number: ____________________

Reason for Visit: ____________________

Questions to Ask: ____________________

____________________

Answers: ____________________

____________________

Concerns? ____________________

____________________

*Lord, watch over me and my precious little one. I trust you and your loving arms to always be around us!*

# Physician's Appointments

Date: ______

Time: ______

Doctors Name and Address: ______

Phone Number: ______ Fax Number: ______

Reason for Visit: ______

Questions to Ask: ______

______

Answers: ______

______

Concerns? ______

______

Date: ______

Time: ______

Doctors Name and Address: ______

Phone Number: ______ Fax Number: ______

Reason for Visit: ______

Questions to Ask: ______

______

Answers: ______

______

Concerns? ______

______

*Lord, watch over me and my precious little one. I trust you and your loving arms to always be around us!*

# Physician's Appointments

Date: __________

Time: __________

Doctors Name and Address: __________

Phone Number: __________ Fax Number: __________

Reason for Visit: __________

Questions to Ask: __________

Answers: __________

Concerns? __________

Date: __________

Time: __________

Doctors Name and Address: __________

Phone Number: __________ Fax Number: __________

Reason for Visit: __________

Questions to Ask: __________

Answers: __________

Concerns? __________

*Lord, watch over me and my precious little one. I trust you and your loving arms to always be around us!*

# Physician's Appointments

Date: ______________________________

Time: ______________________________

Doctors Name and Address: ______________________________

Phone Number: ______________ Fax Number: ______________

Reason for Visit: ______________________________

Questions to Ask: ______________________________

______________________________

Answers: ______________________________

______________________________

Concerns? ______________________________

______________________________

Date: ______________________________

Time: ______________________________

Doctors Name and Address: ______________________________

Phone Number: ______________ Fax Number: ______________

Reason for Visit: ______________________________

Questions to Ask: ______________________________

______________________________

Answers: ______________________________

______________________________

Concerns? ______________________________

______________________________

*Lord, watch over me and my precious little one. I trust you and your loving arms to always be around us!*

# Physician's Appointments

Date: ______

Time: ______

Doctors Name and Address: ______

Phone Number: ______ Fax Number: ______

Reason for Visit: ______

Questions to Ask: ______

______

Answers: ______

______

Concerns? ______

______

Date: ______

Time: ______

Doctors Name and Address: ______

Phone Number: ______ Fax Number: ______

Reason for Visit: ______

Questions to Ask: ______

______

Answers: ______

______

Concerns? ______

______

*Lord, watch over me and my precious little one. I trust you and your loving arms to always be around us!*

# Physician's Appointments

Date: ______

Time: ______

Doctors Name and Address: ______

Phone Number: ______ Fax Number: ______

Reason for Visit: ______

Questions to Ask: ______

______

Answers: ______

______

Concerns? ______

______

Date: ______

Time: ______

Doctors Name and Address: ______

Phone Number: ______ Fax Number: ______

Reason for Visit: ______

Questions to Ask: ______

______

Answers: ______

______

Concerns? ______

______

*Lord, watch over me and my precious little one. I trust you and your loving arms to always be around us!*

# Physician's Appointments

Date: ____________________

Time: ____________________

Doctors Name and Address: ____________________

Phone Number: ____________________ Fax Number: ____________________

Reason for Visit: ____________________

Questions to Ask: ____________________

____________________

Answers: ____________________

____________________

Concerns? ____________________

____________________

Date: ____________________

Time: ____________________

Doctors Name and Address: ____________________

Phone Number: ____________________ Fax Number: ____________________

Reason for Visit: ____________________

Questions to Ask: ____________________

____________________

Answers: ____________________

____________________

Concerns? ____________________

____________________

*Lord, watch over me and my precious little one. I trust you and your loving arms to always be around us!*

# Physician's Appointments

Date: ________________________________

Time: ________________________________

Doctors Name and Address: ________________________

Phone Number: ________________ Fax Number: ________________

Reason for Visit: ____________________________

Questions to Ask: ____________________________

Answers: ________________________________

Concerns? ________________________________

Date: ________________________________

Time: ________________________________

Doctors Name and Address: ________________________

Phone Number: ________________ Fax Number: ________________

Reason for Visit: ____________________________

Questions to Ask: ____________________________

Answers: ________________________________

Concerns? ________________________________

*Lord, watch over me and my precious little one. I trust you and your loving arms to always be around us!*

# Physician's Appointments

Date: ______________________________

Time: ______________________________

Doctors Name and Address: ______________________________

Phone Number: ______________ Fax Number: ______________

Reason for Visit: ______________________________

Questions to Ask: ______________________________

______________________________

Answers: ______________________________

______________________________

Concerns? ______________________________

______________________________

Date: ______________________________

Time: ______________________________

Doctors Name and Address: ______________________________

Phone Number: ______________ Fax Number: ______________

Reason for Visit: ______________________________

Questions to Ask: ______________________________

______________________________

Answers: ______________________________

______________________________

Concerns? ______________________________

______________________________

*Lord, watch over me and my precious little one. I trust you and your loving arms to always be around us!*

# Physician's Appointments

Date: ______

Time: ______

Doctors Name and Address: ______

Phone Number: ______ Fax Number: ______

Reason for Visit: ______

Questions to Ask: ______

______

Answers: ______

______

Concerns? ______

______

Date: ______

Time: ______

Doctors Name and Address: ______

Phone Number: ______ Fax Number: ______

Reason for Visit: ______

Questions to Ask: ______

______

Answers: ______

______

Concerns? ______

______

*Lord, watch over me and my precious little one. I trust you and your loving arms to always be around us!*

# *Physician's Appointments*

Date: ______________________________

Time: ______________________________

Doctors Name and Address: ______________________________

Phone Number: ______________ Fax Number: ______________

Reason for Visit: ______________________________

Questions to Ask: ______________________________

______________________________

Answers: ______________________________

______________________________

Concerns? ______________________________

______________________________

Date: ______________________________

Time: ______________________________

Doctors Name and Address: ______________________________

Phone Number: ______________ Fax Number: ______________

Reason for Visit: ______________________________

Questions to Ask: ______________________________

______________________________

Answers: ______________________________

______________________________

Concerns? ______________________________

______________________________

*Lord, watch over me and my precious little one. I trust you and your loving arms to always be around us!*

# Physician's Appointments

Date: ______________________________

Time: ______________________________

Doctors Name and Address: ______________________________

Phone Number: ______________ Fax Number: ______________

Reason for Visit: ______________________________

Questions to Ask: ______________________________

______________________________

Answers: ______________________________

______________________________

Concerns? ______________________________

______________________________

Date: ______________________________

Time: ______________________________

Doctors Name and Address: ______________________________

Phone Number: ______________ Fax Number: ______________

Reason for Visit: ______________________________

Questions to Ask: ______________________________

______________________________

Answers: ______________________________

______________________________

Concerns? ______________________________

______________________________

*Lord, watch over me and my precious little one. I trust you and your loving arms to always be around us!*

# Physician's Appointments

Date: ______

Time: ______

Doctors Name and Address: ______

Phone Number: ______ Fax Number: ______

Reason for Visit: ______

Questions to Ask: ______

______

Answers: ______

______

Concerns? ______

______

Date: ______

Time: ______

Doctors Name and Address: ______

Phone Number: ______ Fax Number: ______

Reason for Visit: ______

Questions to Ask: ______

______

Answers: ______

______

Concerns? ______

______

*Lord, watch over me and my precious little one. I trust you and your loving arms to always be around us!*

# Physician's Appointments

Date: ______________________________

Time: ______________________________

Doctors Name and Address: ______________________________

Phone Number: ______________ Fax Number: ______________

Reason for Visit: ______________________________

Questions to Ask: ______________________________

______________________________

Answers: ______________________________

______________________________

Concerns? ______________________________

______________________________

Date: ______________________________

Time: ______________________________

Doctors Name and Address: ______________________________

Phone Number: ______________ Fax Number: ______________

Reason for Visit: ______________________________

Questions to Ask: ______________________________

______________________________

Answers: ______________________________

______________________________

Concerns? ______________________________

______________________________

*Lord, watch over me and my precious little one. I trust you and your loving arms to always be around us!*

# *Physician's Appointments*

Date: ______________________________

Time: ______________________________

Doctors Name and Address: ______________________________

Phone Number: ______________ Fax Number: ______________

Reason for Visit: ______________________________

Questions to Ask: ______________________________

______________________________

Answers: ______________________________

______________________________

Concerns? ______________________________

______________________________

Date: ______________________________

Time: ______________________________

Doctors Name and Address: ______________________________

Phone Number: ______________ Fax Number: ______________

Reason for Visit: ______________________________

Questions to Ask: ______________________________

______________________________

Answers: ______________________________

______________________________

Concerns? ______________________________

______________________________

*Lord, watch over me and my precious little one. I trust you and your loving arms to always be around us!*

# Baby Names

**My choices for names if my baby is a boy**

First name: ______________________ Middle name: ______________________

First name: ______________________ Middle name: ______________________

First name: ______________________ Middle name: ______________________

**Top 100 Most Popular boys names**

*(per the SSA website date http://www.ssa.gov/cgi-binpopularnames.cgi)*

**Jacob** . . . . . . . . Hebrew . . . . . . . . Supplanter
**Ethan** . . . . . . . . Hebrew . . . . . . . . Strong, Firm
**Michael** . . . . . . Hebrew . . . . . . . . Who is like God
**Jayden** . . . . . . . American . . . . . . . Grateful
**William** . . . . . . Germanic . . . . . . . Will/Desire/Protection
**Alexander** . . . . . Greek . . . . . . . . . Defender
**Noah** . . . . . . . . Hebrew . . . . . . . . Rest/Comfort
**Daniel** . . . . . . . Hebrew . . . . . . . . God is My Judge
**Aiden** . . . . . . . . Gaelic . . . . . . . . . Little fire
**Anthony** . . . . . . Latin. . . . . . . . . . Priceless
**Joshua** . . . . . . . Hebrew . . . . . . . . God Rescues
**Mason** . . . . . . . French . . . . . . . . Bricklayer
**Christopher** . . . . Greek . . . . . . . . . Bearer of Christ
**Andrew** . . . . . . . Greek . . . . . . . . . Man/warrior
**David** . . . . . . . . Hebrew . . . . . . . . Beloved
**Matthew** . . . . . . Hebrew . . . . . . . . Gift of God
**Logan** . . . . . . . . Gaelic . . . . . . . . . Hollow
**Elijah** . . . . . . . . Hebrew . . . . . . . . My God is the lord
**James** . . . . . . . . Hebrew . . . . . . . . Supplanter
**Joseph** . . . . . . . Hebrew . . . . . . . . He will enlarge
**Gabriel** . . . . . . . Hebrew . . . . . . . . God is my might
**Benjamin** . . . . . Hebrew . . . . . . . . Son of my right hand
**Ryan** . . . . . . . . Gaelic . . . . . . . . . Little King

| | | |
|---|---|---|
| **Samuel** | Hebrew | His name is God |
| **Jackson** | English | Jack's son |
| **John** | Hebrew | God is gracious |
| **Nathan** | Hebrew | God has given |
| **Jonathan** | Hebrew | God has given |
| **Christian** | Latin. | Follower of Christ |
| **Liam** | Germanic | Will/desire/protection |
| **Dylan** | Welsh | god of the sea |
| **Landon** | English | Long hill |
| **Caleb** | Hebrew | Dog/heart |
| **Tyler** | English | Tile maker |
| **Lucas** | Greek | Man from Lucania |
| **Evan** | Hebrew | God is gracious |
| **Gavin** | Welsh | White hawk of battle |
| **Nicholas** | Greek | Victory of the people |
| **Isaac** | Greek | He will laugh |
| **Brayden** | English | Broad/wide |
| **Luke** | Greek | Man from Lucania |
| **Angel** | Greek | Messenger |
| **Brandon** | English | Broom hill |
| **Jack** | Hebrew | God is gracious |
| **Isaiah** | Hebrew | God is salvation |
| **Jordan** | Hebrew | Descend/flow down |
| **Owen** | Gaelic | Well born |
| **Carter** | English | Transporter of materials |
| **Connor** | Gaelic | Lover of hounds |
| **Justin** | Latin. | Righteous/just |
| **Jose** | Hebrew | He will enlarge |
| **Jeremiah** | Hebrew | God will raise up |
| **Julian** | Latin. | Down-bearded youth |
| **Robert** | Germanic | Bright fame |
| **Aaron** | Hebrew | Mountain |
| **Adrian** | Latin. | From Hadria |
| **Wyatt** | English | Brave/strong/hardy |
| **Kevin** | Gaelic | Beautiful at birth |
| **Hunter** | English | Hunter/one who hunts |
| **Cameron** | Gaelic | Crooked nose |
| **Zachary** | Hebrew | The Lord remembers |
| **Thomas** | Aramaic | Twin |

| Name | Origin | Meaning |
|---|---|---|
| **Charles** | Germanic | Free man |
| **Austin** | Latin | Venerated |
| **Eli** | Hebrew | Ascend/my God |
| **Chase** | English | Huntsman |
| **Henry** | Germanic | Home ruler |
| **Sebastian** | Latin | Made from Sebaste |
| **Jason** | Greek | Healer |
| **Levi** | Hebrew | Heart |
| **Xavier** | Basque | New House |
| **Ian** | Hebrew | God is Forgiving |
| **Colton** | English | Coal Town |
| **Dominic** | Latin | Lord |
| **Juan** | Hebrew | God is gracious |
| **Cooper** | English | Barrel-maker |
| **Josiah** | Hebrew | The Lord Saves |
| **Louis** | Germanic | Fame and war |
| **Ayden** | Gaelic | Little fire |
| **Carson** | Gaelic | from Carson |
| **Adam** | Hebrew | Man/earth |
| **Nathaniel** | Hebrew | Gift of God |
| **Brody** | Gaelic | Muddy Place |
| **Tristan** | Gaelic | Tumult |
| **Diego** | Hebrew | Supplanter |
| **Parker** | English | Gamekeeper |
| **Blake** | English | Dark/bright |
| **Oliver** | French | Elf army |
| **Cole** | English | Coal/dark one |
| **Carlos** | German | free man |
| **Jaden** | American | Grateful |
| **Jesus** | Hebrew | God rescues |
| **Alex** | Greek | Defending men |
| **Aidan** | Gaelic | Little fire |
| **Eric** | Norse | Eternal ruler |
| **Hayden** | German | Heathen |
| **Bryan** | Gaelic | Noble/strong |
| **Max** | Latin | The greatest |
| **Jaxon** | English | Jack's son |
| **Brian** | Gaelic | Noble/strong |

# Baby Names

**My choices for names if my baby is a girl**

First name: ______________ Middle name: ______________

First name: ______________ Middle name: ______________

First name: ______________ Middle name: ______________

**Top 100 Most Popular girls names**

*(per the SSA website date http://www.ssa.gov/cgi-binpopularnames.cgi)*

| | | |
|---|---|---|
| **Isabella** | Hebrew | My God is a vow |
| **Sophia** | Greek | Wisdom |
| **Emma** | German | All-containing |
| **Olivia** | English | Elf-army |
| **Ava** | Afghan | Voice |
| **Emily** | Latin | Rival/emulating |
| **Abigail** | Hebrew | Father in rejoicing |
| **Madison** | English | Son of Maud/Matthew |
| **Chloe** | Greek | Young shoot |
| **Mia** | Danish | Pet form of Maria |
| **Addison** | English | Son of Adam |
| **Elizabeth** | Hebrew | My God is a vow |
| **Ella** | Greek | Torch/bright light |
| **Natalie** | Italian | Christ's birthday |
| **Samantha** | Aramaic | Listener |
| **Alexis** | Greek | Defender |
| **Lily** | English | Lily/flower |
| **Grace** | Latin | Good Will |
| **Hailey** | English | Hay clearing |
| **Alyssa** | Germanic | Noble/kind |
| **Lillian** | Hebrew | My God is a vow/lillies |
| **Hannah** | Hebrew | Grace/favor |
| **Avery** | English | Elf counsel |

| Name | Origin | Meaning |
|---|---|---|
| **Leah** | Hebrew | Weary |
| **Nevaeh** | American | Heaven spelled backwards |
| **Sophia** | Greek | Wisdom |
| **Ashley** | English | Ash wood |
| **Anna** | Hebrew | Grace/favor |
| **Brianna** | Gaelic | Noble/strong |
| **Sarah** | Hebrew | Princess |
| **Zoe** | Greek | Life |
| **Victoria** | Latin | Conqueror/victory |
| **Gabriella** | Hebrew | God is my might |
| **Brooklyn** | Dutch | broken land |
| **Kaylee** | Gaelic | Descendant of Caollaidhe |
| **Taylor** | English | A tailor |
| **Layla** | Arabic | Dark beauty |
| **Allison** | Germanic | Noble/kind |
| **Evelyn** | Hebrew | Life |
| **Riley** | English | Rye cleaning |
| **Amelia** | Germanic | Work/effort/strain |
| **Khloe** | Greek | Young Shoot |
| **Makayla** | Hebrew | Who is like God |
| **Aubrey** | Germanic | Elfin King |
| **Charlotte** | Germanic | Free man |
| **Savannah** | Spanish | Plateau |
| **Zoey** | Greek | Life |
| **Bella** | Italian | Beautiful |
| **Kayla** | Hebrew | Who is like God |
| **Alexa** | Greek | Defending men |
| **Peyton** | English | Settlement of Paga |
| **Audrey** | English | Noble strength |
| **Claire** | Hebrew | Grace/Favor |
| **Arianna** | Greek | Very holy one |
| **Julia** | Latin | Down-bearded youth |
| **Aaliyah** | Arabic | Lofty/sublime |
| **Kylie** | Pacific Islands | Boomerang |
| **Lauren** | Latin | Man from Laurentum |
| **Sophie** | Greek | Wisdom |
| **Sydney** | English | Wide Meadow |
| **Camila** | Latin | Altar server |
| **Jasmine** | Persian | Jasmine/flower |

**Morgan** . . . . . . . .Welsh . . . . . . . . . .Bright sea
**Alexandra** . . . . .Greek . . . . . . . . . .Defending men
**Jocelyn** . . . . . . . .French . . . . . . . . . .Tribal name of the Gauts
**Gianna** . . . . . . .Hebrew . . . . . . . . .God is gracious
**Maya** . . . . . . . . .Sanskrit . . . . . . . . .Illusion
**Kimberly** . . . . . .English . . . . . . . . .Forest clearing
**Mackenzie** . . . . .Gaelic . . . . . . . . . .Son of Coinneach
**Katherine** . . . . .Greek . . . . . . . . . .Pure
**Destiny** . . . . . . .English . . . . . . . . .Destiny/fate
**Brooke** . . . . . . .English . . . . . . . . .A brook/stream
**Trinity** . . . . . . .Latin . . . . . . . . . . .Threefold
**Faith** . . . . . . . .English . . . . . . . . .Faith/confidence
**Lucy** . . . . . . . . .Latin . . . . . . . . . . .Light
**Madelyn** . . . . . .Hebrew . . . . . . . . .From Magdala
**Madeline** . . . . .Hebrew . . . . . . . . .From Magdala
**Bailey** . . . . . . . .English . . . . . . . . .Bailiff
**Payton** . . . . . . .English . . . . . . . . .Settlement of Paga
**Andrea** . . . . . . .Greek . . . . . . . . . .Man warrior
**Autumn** . . . . . .English . . . . . . . . .Autumn/fall season
**Melanie** . . . . . .Greek . . . . . . . . . .Black
**Ariana** . . . . . . .Greek . . . . . . . . . .Very holy one
**Serenity** . . . . . .English . . . . . . . . .Peacefulness
**Stella** . . . . . . . .Latin . . . . . . . . . . .Star
**Maria** . . . . . . . .Hebrew . . . . . . . . .Bitter
**Molly** . . . . . . . .English . . . . . . . . .Pet form of Mary
**Caroline** . . . . . .German . . . . . . . . .Free man
**Genesis** . . . . . . .Hebrew . . . . . . . . .Beginning/birth
**Kaitlyn** . . . . . . .Gaelic . . . . . . . . . .Pure
**Eva** . . . . . . . . . .Hebrew . . . . . . . . .Life
**Jessica** . . . . . . .Literary . . . . . . . . .Character/Shakespeare
**Angelina** . . . . . .Greek . . . . . . . . . .Messenger
**Valeria** . . . . . . .Latin . . . . . . . . . . .To be healthy/strong
**Garbrielle** . . . . .Hebrew . . . . . . . . .God is my might
**Naomi** . . . . . . . .Hebrew . . . . . . . . .Beautiful/delightful
**Mariah** . . . . . . .Hebrew . . . . . . . . .Bitter
**Natalia** . . . . . . .Italian . . . . . . . . . .Christ's birthday
**Paige** . . . . . . . .English . . . . . . . . .Page
**Rachel** . . . . . . . .Hebrew . . . . . . . . .Ewe

# My Baby Shower

Date and Time: ______________________________

Location:

______________________________

______________________________

Who attended:

______________________________

______________________________

______________________________

______________________________

______________________________

______________________________

______________________________

______________________________

______________________________

______________________________

______________________________

Games played:

______________________________

______________________________

______________________________

______________________________

______________________________

Special foods and highlights:

______________________________

______________________________

______________________________

______________________________

# *Gifts Received*

Gift ___

*Given by* ___

Gift ___

*Given by* ___

Gift ___

*Given by* ___

Gift ___

*Given by* ___

Gift ___

*Given by* ___

Gift ___

*Given by* ___

Gift ___

*Given by* ___

Gift ___

*Given by* ___

Gift ___

*Given by* ___

*Thank you God for all the good and perfect gifts you give to me, but most of all, I thank you for the precious gift of my baby!*

# Baby Nursery and Gear

Baby's Nursery décor ideas

Colors I like:

Patterns or themes I like:

Websites to check out:

# What I will need for Baby's nursery and On-the-go

**Nursery Necessities**

- ☐ crib and crib mattress
- ☐ fitted sheets and bumper
- ☐ cabinet or shelf to store baby's clothes and supplies
- ☐ changing table and changing pad
- ☐ diaper pail
- ☐ night light

**Bathing and Hygiene**

- ☐ diapers newborn size
- ☐ baby wipes
- ☐ antibiotic ointment
- ☐ diaper rash cream
- ☐ nasal aspirator
- ☐ infant nail clippers
- ☐ baby wash and tearless baby shampoo
- ☐ petroleum jelly
- ☐ thermometer
- ☐ baby towel and baby bathtub

**Clothes for Baby**

- ☐ outfit for baby to wear home
- ☐ socks/booties
- ☐ onesies
- ☐ receiving blankets
- ☐ sleepers
- ☐ hats to keep head warm

**Baby-on-the-go**

- ☐ infant car seat
- ☐ diaper bag
- ☐ portable changing pad
- ☐ stroller

**Baby Feeding supplies**

- ☐ bibs
- ☐ bottles
- ☐ nipples
- ☐ bottle and nipple brush
- ☐ sterilizer for bottles/nipples/pacifiers

**Extras**

- ☐ nursery monitor
- ☐ portable crib
- ☐ rocking chair
- ☐ baby swing

## My Bags are packed and I'm ready for Delivery Day!

**Hospital bag checklist**

*Try to have as many of these items ready and in your bag in a safe place that you and your partner know where it is so you can "grab-n-go!"*

- ☐ Insurance card
- ☐ cell phone and charger
- ☐ this organizer journal!
- ☐ changing table and changing pad
- ☐ toiletries (toothbrush, toothpaste, deodorant, hair brush, hair ties, lip balm, lotion, makeup)
- ☐ maternity undies (2 to 3 pairs)
- ☐ feminine pads (heavy-flow)
- ☐ non-slip socks
- ☐ robe or gown
- ☐ healthy snacks
- ☐ paper and pen
- ☐ camera
- ☐ maternity outfit to wear home
- ☐ baby's homecoming outfit
- ☐ thermometer

Other extras to put on your own personal list...

______________________________

______________________________

______________________________

______________________________

______________________________

______________________________

**Make sure to have your infant car seat purchased and ready before you leave for the hospital.**

# Delivery Day Events

Date I went to the hospital: ____________________

Hospital name: ____________________

Location: ____________________

Arrival time: ____________________

How did I know I was in labor? ____________________

____________________

Doctor's name: ____________________

Doctor's phone number: ____________________

Nurse(s) name: ____________________

Who was with me? ____________________

My emotions: ____________________

____________________

____________________

____________________

Lord I pray for your protection and guidance through the delivery, and health for my baby

*For He shall give His angels charge over you,*
*to keep you in all your ways.*

PSALM 91:11 NKJV

## Contractions Started

| TIME START | TIME FINISH | DESCRIBE<br>*Tolerable, Ouch, Break-a-sweat,<br>OMG! (Oh My Goodness!)* |
|---|---|---|
| | | |
| | | |
| | | |
| | | |
| | | |
| | | |
| | | |
| | | |
| | | |
| | | |
| | | |
| | | |
| | | |
| | | |
| | | |
| | | |
| | | |
| | | |
| | | |
| | | |
| | | |
| | | |
| | | |
| | | |
| | | |
| | | |
| | | |

# Important Phone Numbers for Delivery Day

Doctor: __________

Grandparents: __________

Baby sitter: __________

Baby sitter alternate: __________

**Other important people to call:**

Name: __________ Phone: __________

Name: __________ Phone: __________

Name: __________ Phone: __________

Name: __________ Phone: __________

Name: __________ Phone: __________

Name: __________ Phone: __________

Name: __________ Phone: __________

Name: __________ Phone: __________

Name: __________ Phone: __________

Name: __________ Phone: __________

Name: __________ Phone: __________

Name: __________ Phone: __________

Name: __________ Phone: __________

# *Welcome Baby!*

# *Here I am!*

Baby's Full name:

________________________________________

Weight: ____________________ Length: ____________________

Date and Time of Birth:

________________________________________

Hair Color: ____________________ Eye Color: ____________________

Birthmarks:

________________________________________

*Special comments about first sounds or moments in the delivery room:*

________________________________________

________________________________________

________________________________________

*Who held baby first:*

________________________________________

The first time I heard your cry, the first sound from your mouth, it was music to my ears!

*Let every living thing that has breath praise the LORD!*

PSALM 150:6 NKJV

# Baby's Family Tree

Baby's name:

Mother's name:

Father's name:

Maternal Grandmother:

Maternal Grandfather:

Paternal Grandmother:

Paternal Grandfather:

Brothers and Sisters:

# People who came to visit me in the hospital

# *Gifts and flowers received while in the hospital*

# Baby's Footprints

*For You formed my inward parts; You covered me in my mother's womb. I will praise You, for I am fearfully and wonderfully made. Marvelous are Your works, and That my soul knows very well.*

PSALM 139:13, 14 NKJV